GRAPHIC TALES OF THE SUPERNATURAL

ZOMBIES

TALES OF THE LIVING DEAD

by Rob Shone

rosen publishing's
rosen
central®

New York

Published in 2011 by The Rosen Publishing Group, Inc.
29 East 21st Street, New York, NY 10010

First edition, 2011

Designed and produced by
David West Books

Photo credits:
4t/4m, Doron; 4b, James G. Pinsky/U.S. Navy; 5t, H. Zell.

 Library of Congress Cataloging-in-Publication Data

 Shone, Rob.
 Zombies : tales of the living dead / Rob Shone. -- 1st ed.
    p. cm. -- (Graphic tales of the supernatural)
 Includes bibliographical references and index.
 ISBN 978-1-4488-1904-1 (library binding) -- ISBN 978-1-4488-1907-2 (pbk.) -- ISBN 978-1-4488-1916-4 (6-pack)
 1. Zombies--Comic books, strips, etc. I. Title.
 BF1556.S565 2010
 398.21--dc22

                                        2010025861

Manufactured in China

CPSIA Compliance Information Batch #DW1102YA:
For further information contact Rosen Publishing, New York, New York, at 1-800-237-9932.

CONTENTS

THE WORLD OF THE ZOMBIE

Zombies are commonplace in Haiti, or so the people there will tell you. Haitians themselves are not afraid of zombies—but they are afraid of becoming one!

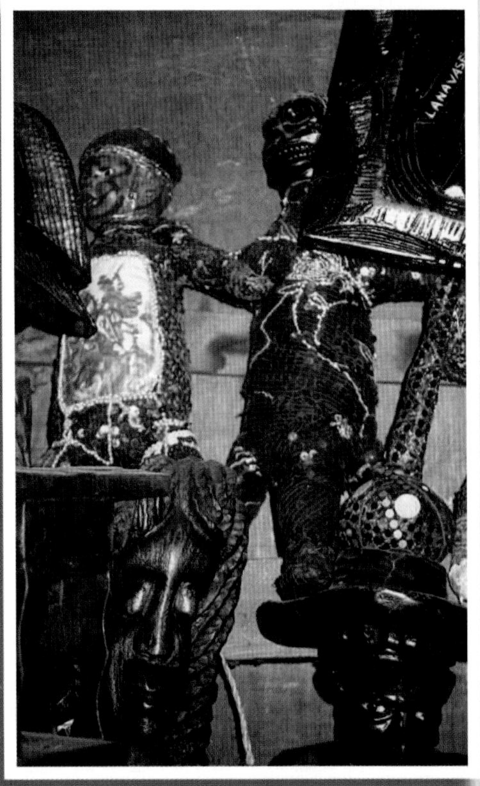

Voodoo totems and charms on sale in a Port-au-Prince shop

Zombie Beginnings

In the 16th century slaves from West Africa were brought to Haiti. Their African religious beliefs traveled with them. Those beliefs are known as Voodoo. There are two types of Voodoo. Rado Voodoo is peaceful and helpful while Petro Voodoo is perceived as darker and more dangerous. This is the Voodoo of the bokors, the sorcerer priests who create zombies.

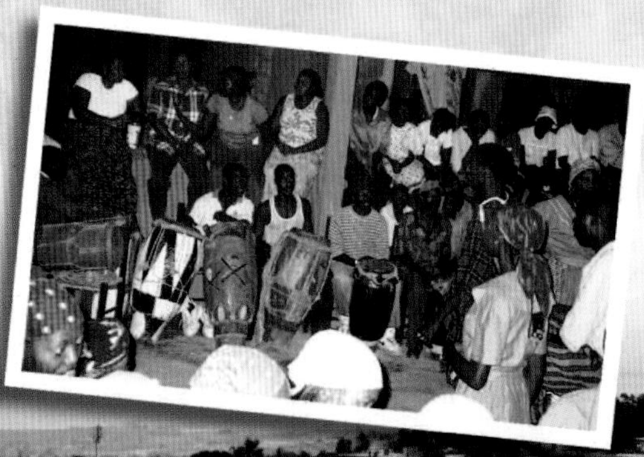

A Voodoo ceremony (left) being performed in the Haitian town of Jacmel

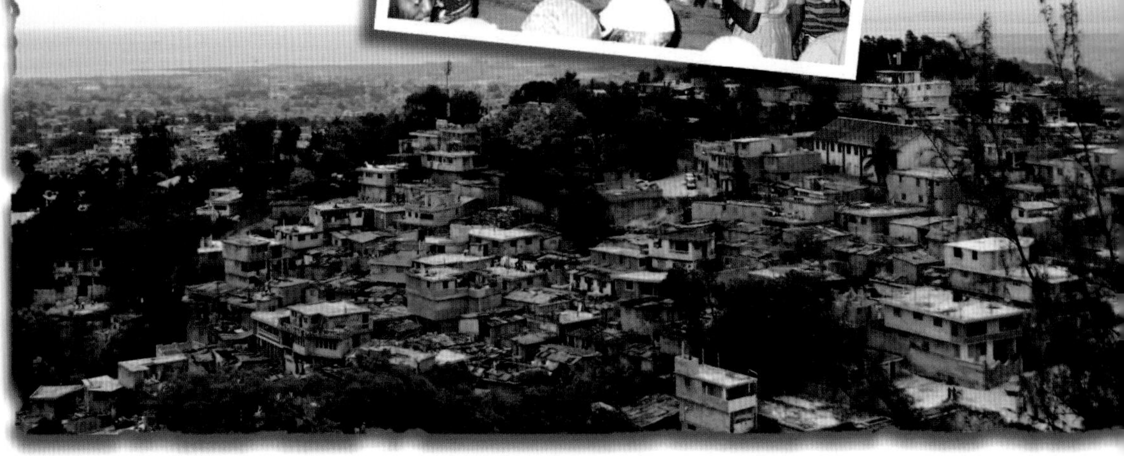

Port-au-Prince (below) is the capital of Haiti. Creating a zombie is illegal in Haiti.

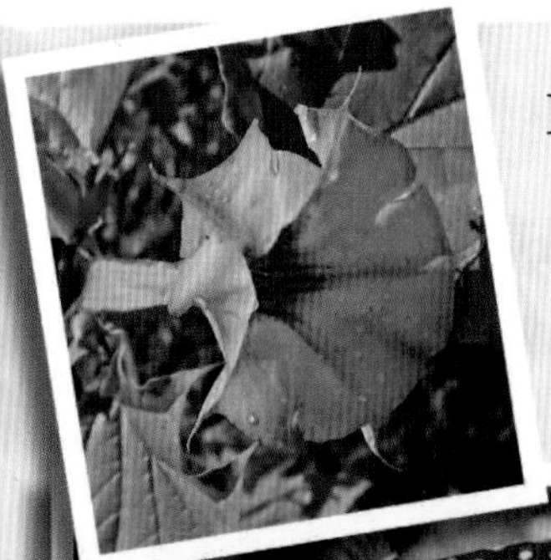

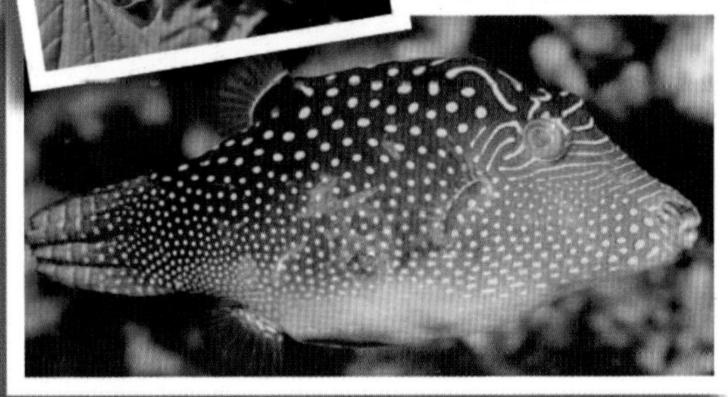

The Datura plant (top) and the Puffer fish both contain drugs that might be used to create zombies.

How to Make a Zombie

In 1982, Canadian scientist, Wade Davis, went to Haiti to investigate whether drugs played a part in creating zombies. When he analyzed a zombie potion, he found that it contained tetrodotoxin, a poison found in puffer fish. Tetrodotoxin paralyzes the body and could bring on the appearance of death. To keep a victim in a zombie state, a bokor would feed them a paste made from the Datura plant, a source of the powerful mind-controlling drug, scopolamine.

Zombies and Popular Culture

In the 1920s zombies started to appear in works of fiction. Authors such as H.P. Lovecraft and W.B. Seabrook featured them in novels and short stories. Then, in 1932, *White Zombie*, the first zombie film, was produced. In these early books and films zombies were portrayed as slow, mindless thugs under the control of an evil witch doctor or mad scientist. In 1968 this image changed with George A. Romero's film *Night of the Living Dead*. Romero's zombies were decaying cannibals that could only be stopped by chopping off their heads. These new zombies did not need a Voodoo bokor to create them. A victim could be zombified simply by being bitten by one.

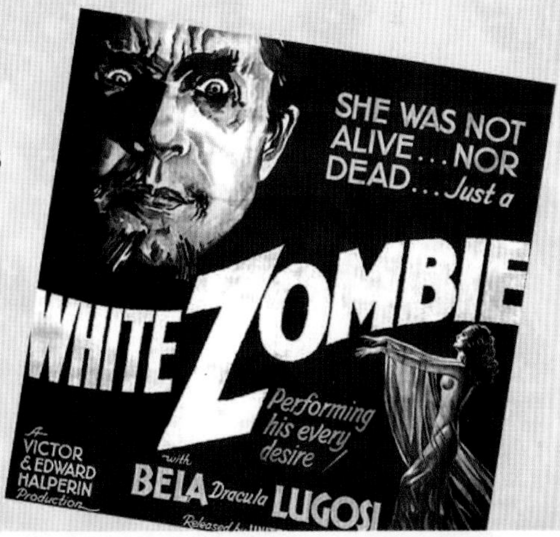
SHE WAS NOT ALIVE...NOR DEAD...Just a
WHITE ZOMBIE
Performing his every desire
A VICTOR & EDWARD HALPERIN Production
with
BELA Dracula LUGOSI

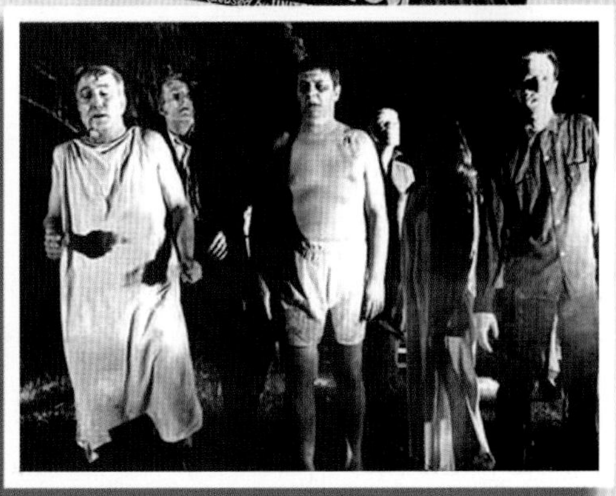

A poster (top) for the film White Zombie, *starring Bela Lugosi*
A still (above) from Night of the Living Dead

A QUICK GUIDE TO THE UNDEAD

Cemeteries, tombs, crypts, and graves are where the dead are laid to rest, and also where the dead can be brought back to life again. Whether they have a mind of their own or not, the undead are all intent on mischief—and worse.

KEEPING THE UNDEAD DEAD

The Ancient Greeks called it "maschalismos," making sure the dead stayed dead. Greek murder victims might have their hands, feet, ears, and nose cut off, strung together like a necklace, and tied under the armpits. In the Maluku Islands of Indonesia, a corpse may have pins stuck into its joints and an egg placed under its chin. In Europe, bodies could be buried upside down, or stones piled onto the coffin lid. A stake could be driven through a likely revenant's heart, or its body might be chopped up and burned. Big toes are sometimes tied together, or the head cut off and placed between the knees.

This woodcut depicts skeletons rising from their graves and performing the Dance of Death. Steps lead down to a church crypt (below). Many stories of the undead begin in places like this.

A gashadokuro (below) is summoned by a sorceress. A sea draugr (bottom) sits in a boat, much to the crew's alarm.

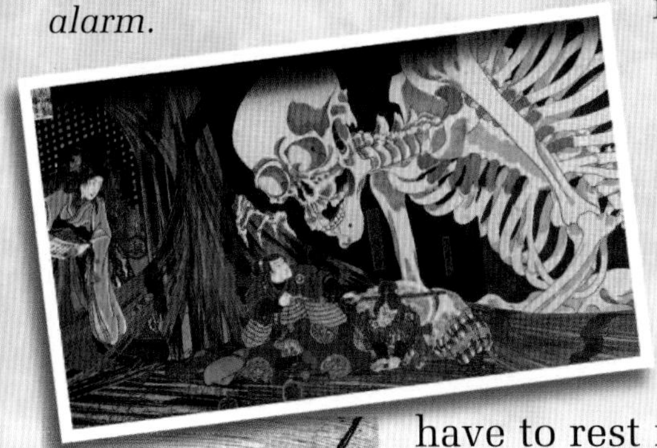

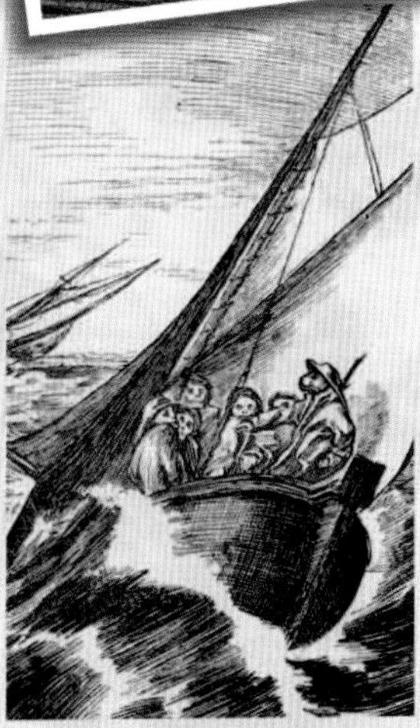

TYPES OF UNDEAD

Revenants–The name comes from the French for "to return." A revenant has usually led a wicked life and has risen from the dead to terrorize the living.

Draugr–These Scandinavian monsters live in the graves of Viking warriors. Sea draugen have heads made of seaweed.

Vrykolaka–Greek vrykolakas have to rest in their graves on Saturdays, which is when they are most vulnerable.

Jiang Shi–In China, if a person's soul does not leave the body after death, they can become a jiang shi. They move about by hopping with their arms stretched out before them. They do not stop rotting, so over time they look increasingly horrific.

Gashadokuro–These Japanese skeletons, many times bigger than a man, are made from the bones of people who have died from hunger. They bite the heads off anyone they can catch.

Vampires–The undisputed kings and queens of the undead, vampires have been around as long as people. These blood suckers can be found throughout the world.

Mummies–Not really one of the undead, "reborn" mummies are largely a creation of the Hollywood film industry.

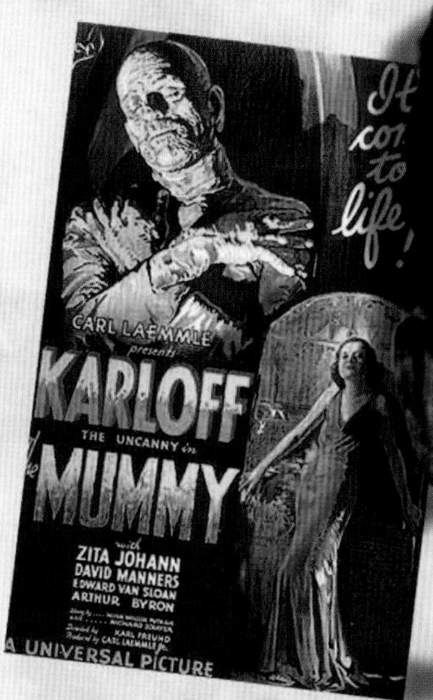
CARL LAEMMLE
presents
KARLOFF
THE UNCANNY in
MUMMY
with
ZITA JOHANN
DAVID MANNERS
EDWARD VAN SLOAN
ARTHUR BYRON
A UNIVERSAL PICTURE

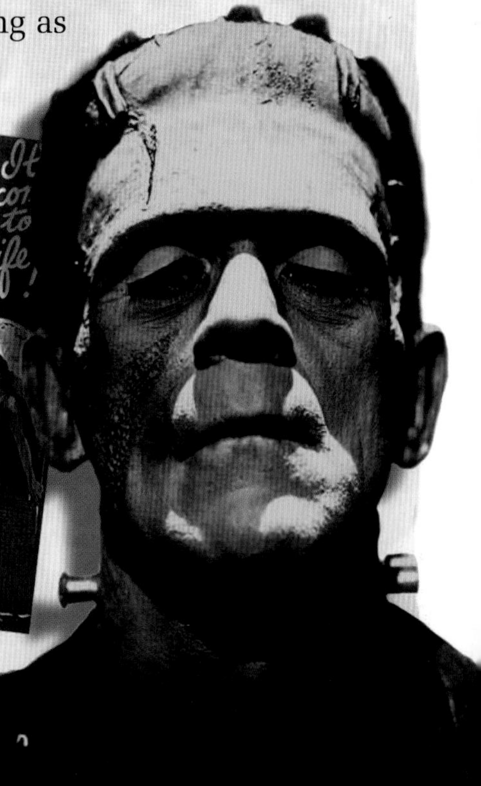

A poster for the film The Mummy *and (right) Frankenstein's monster from the film* Frankenstein *–both these undead creatures began life as works of literary fiction.*

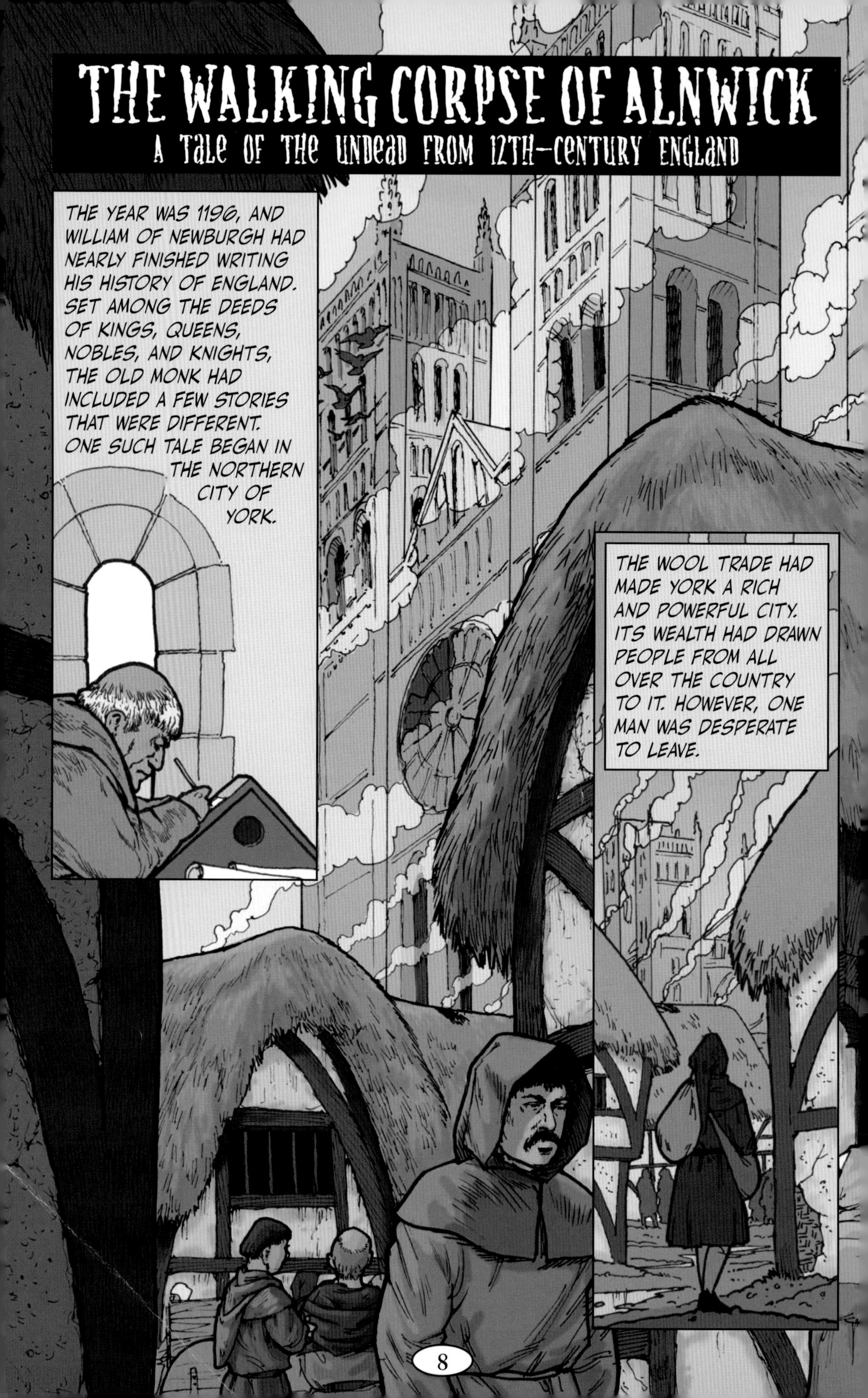
THE WALKING CORPSE OF ALNWICK
A TALE OF THE UNDEAD FROM 12TH-CENTURY ENGLAND
THE YEAR WAS 1196, AND WILLIAM OF NEWBURGH HAD NEARLY FINISHED WRITING HIS HISTORY OF ENGLAND. SET AMONG THE DEEDS OF KINGS, QUEENS, NOBLES, AND KNIGHTS, THE OLD MONK HAD INCLUDED A FEW STORIES THAT WERE DIFFERENT. ONE SUCH TALE BEGAN IN THE NORTHERN CITY OF YORK.
THE WOOL TRADE HAD MADE YORK A RICH AND POWERFUL CITY. ITS WEALTH HAD DRAWN PEOPLE FROM ALL OVER THE COUNTRY TO IT. HOWEVER, ONE MAN WAS DESPERATE TO LEAVE.

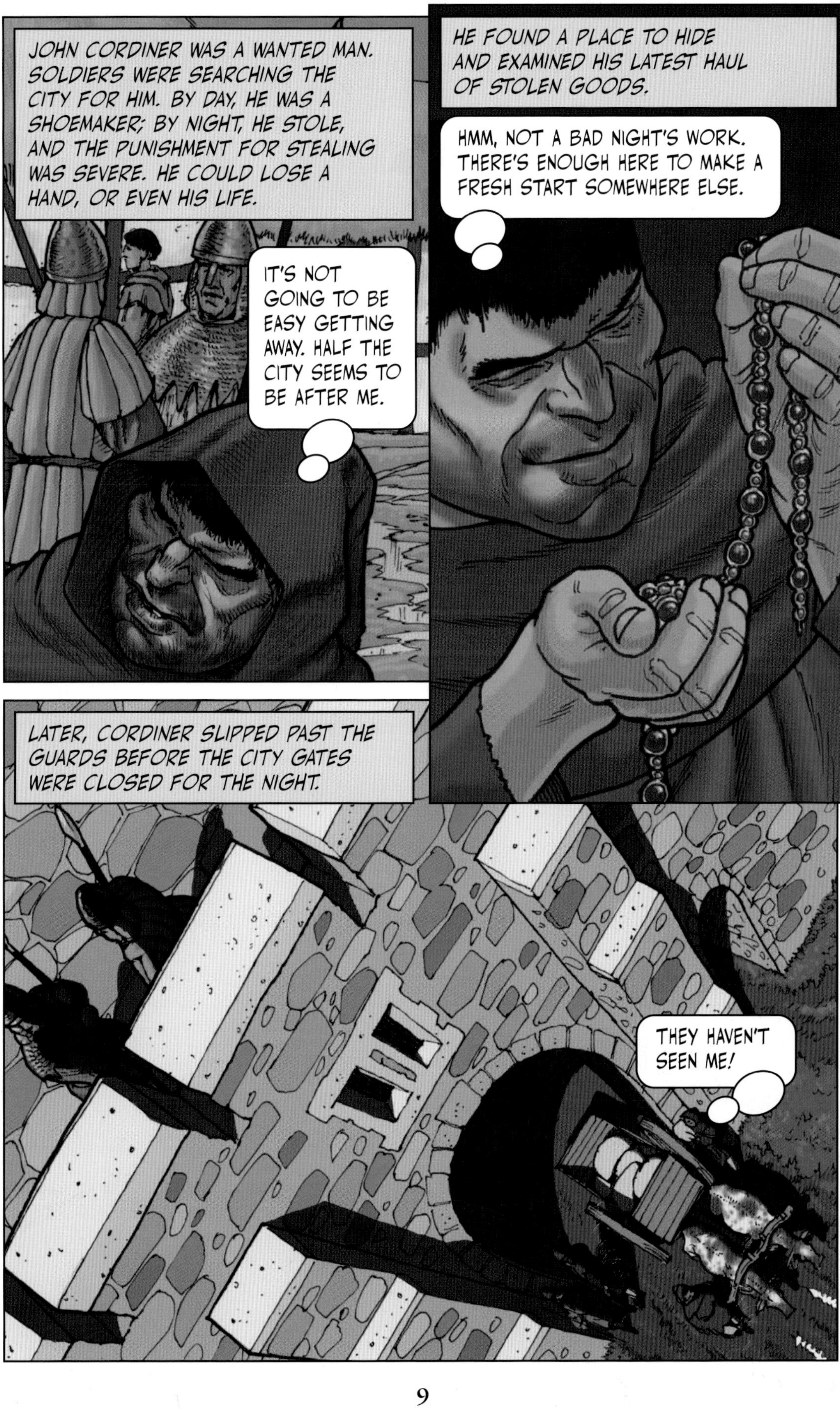
JOHN CORDINER WAS A WANTED MAN. SOLDIERS WERE SEARCHING THE CITY FOR HIM. BY DAY, HE WAS A SHOEMAKER; BY NIGHT, HE STOLE, AND THE PUNISHMENT FOR STEALING WAS SEVERE. HE COULD LOSE A HAND, OR EVEN HIS LIFE.
IT'S NOT GOING TO BE EASY GETTING AWAY. HALF THE CITY SEEMS TO BE AFTER ME.
HE FOUND A PLACE TO HIDE AND EXAMINED HIS LATEST HAUL OF STOLEN GOODS.
HMM, NOT A BAD NIGHT'S WORK. THERE'S ENOUGH HERE TO MAKE A FRESH START SOMEWHERE ELSE.
LATER, CORDINER SLIPPED PAST THE GUARDS BEFORE THE CITY GATES WERE CLOSED FOR THE NIGHT.
THEY HAVEN'T SEEN ME!

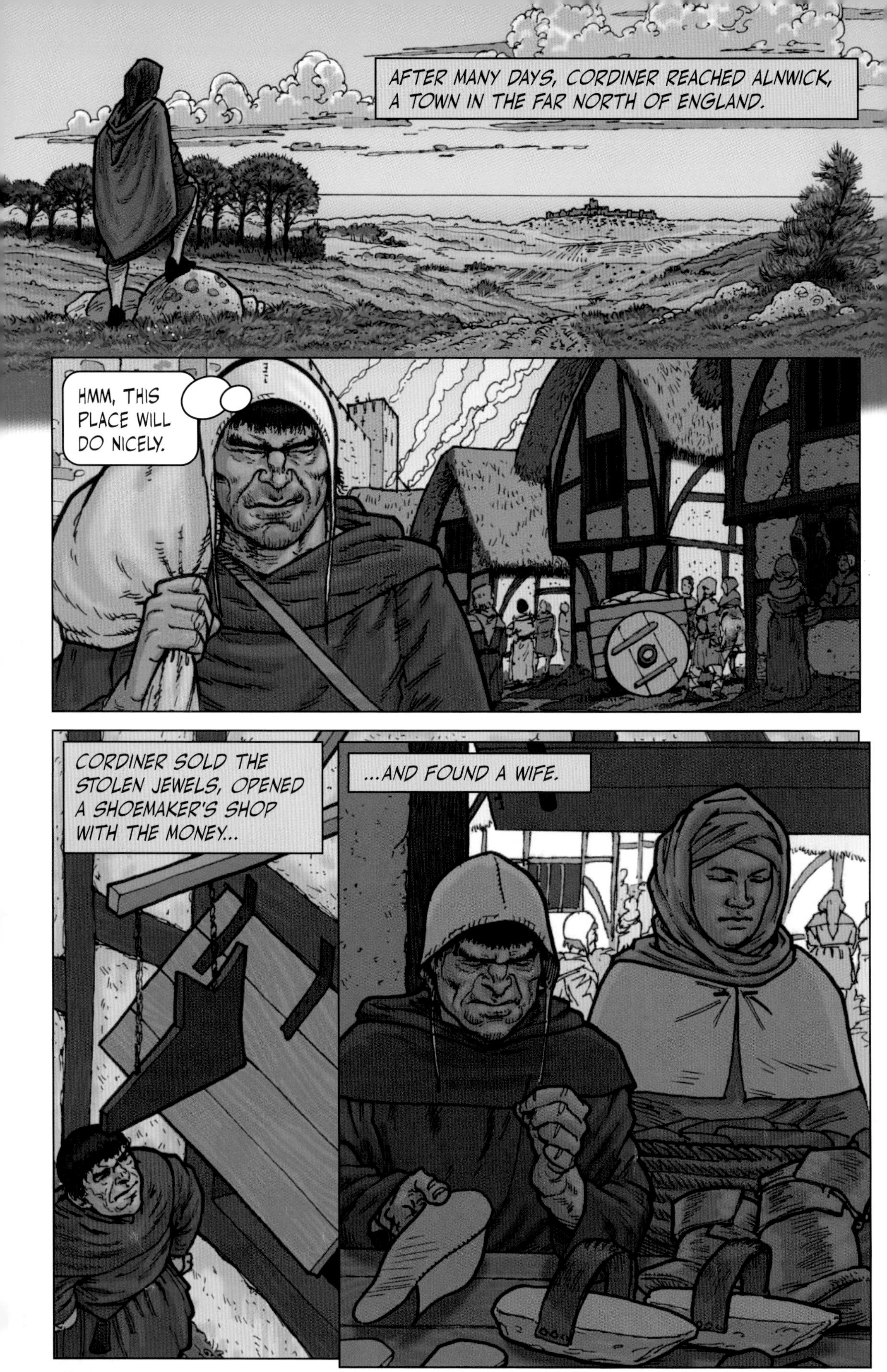
AFTER MANY DAYS, CORDINER REACHED ALNWICK, A TOWN IN THE FAR NORTH OF ENGLAND.
HMM, THIS PLACE WILL DO NICELY.
CORDINER SOLD THE STOLEN JEWELS, OPENED A SHOEMAKER'S SHOP WITH THE MONEY...
...AND FOUND A WIFE.

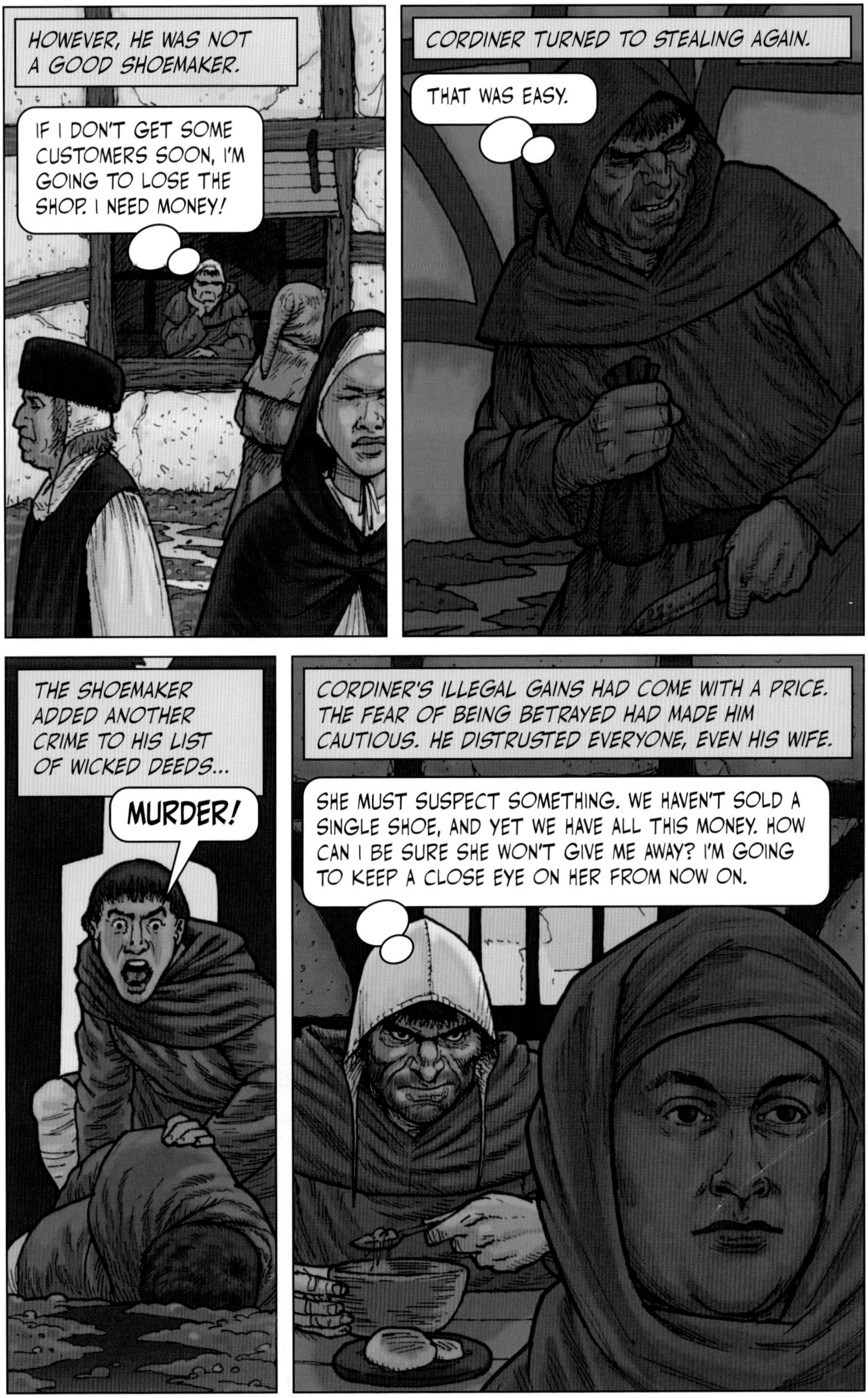
HOWEVER, HE WAS NOT A GOOD SHOEMAKER.
IF I DON'T GET SOME CUSTOMERS SOON, I'M GOING TO LOSE THE SHOP. I NEED MONEY!
CORDINER TURNED TO STEALING AGAIN.
THAT WAS EASY.
THE SHOEMAKER ADDED ANOTHER CRIME TO HIS LIST OF WICKED DEEDS...
MURDER!
CORDINER'S ILLEGAL GAINS HAD COME WITH A PRICE. THE FEAR OF BEING BETRAYED HAD MADE HIM CAUTIOUS. HE DISTRUSTED EVERYONE, EVEN HIS WIFE.
SHE MUST SUSPECT SOMETHING. WE HAVEN'T SOLD A SINGLE SHOE, AND YET WE HAVE ALL THIS MONEY. HOW CAN I BE SURE SHE WON'T GIVE ME AWAY? I'M GOING TO KEEP A CLOSE EYE ON HER FROM NOW ON.

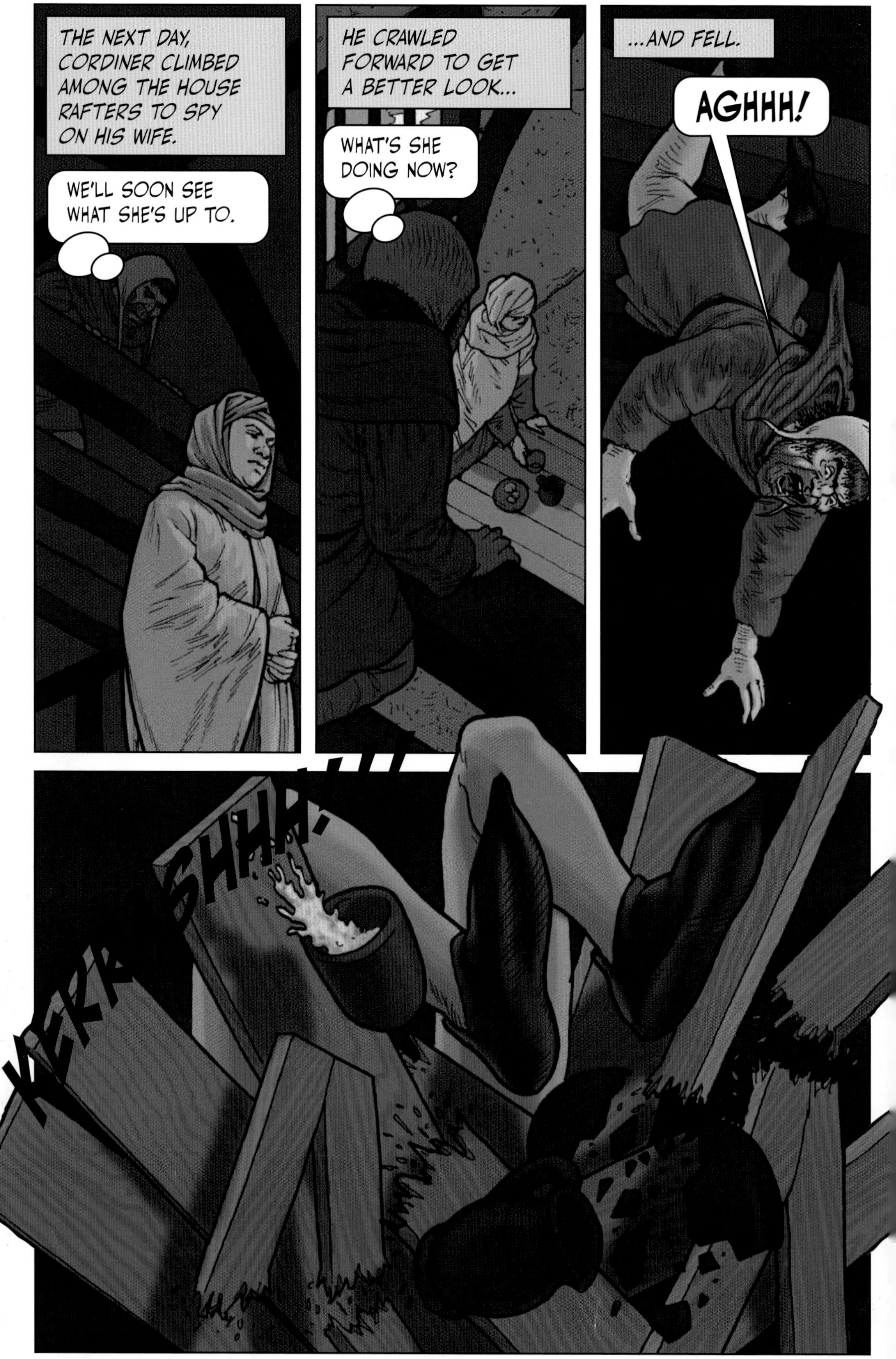
THE NEXT DAY, CORDINER CLIMBED AMONG THE HOUSE RAFTERS TO SPY ON HIS WIFE.
WE'LL SOON SEE WHAT SHE'S UP TO.
HE CRAWLED FORWARD TO GET A BETTER LOOK...
WHAT'S SHE DOING NOW?
...AND FELL.
AGHHH!
KERRASHH!!!

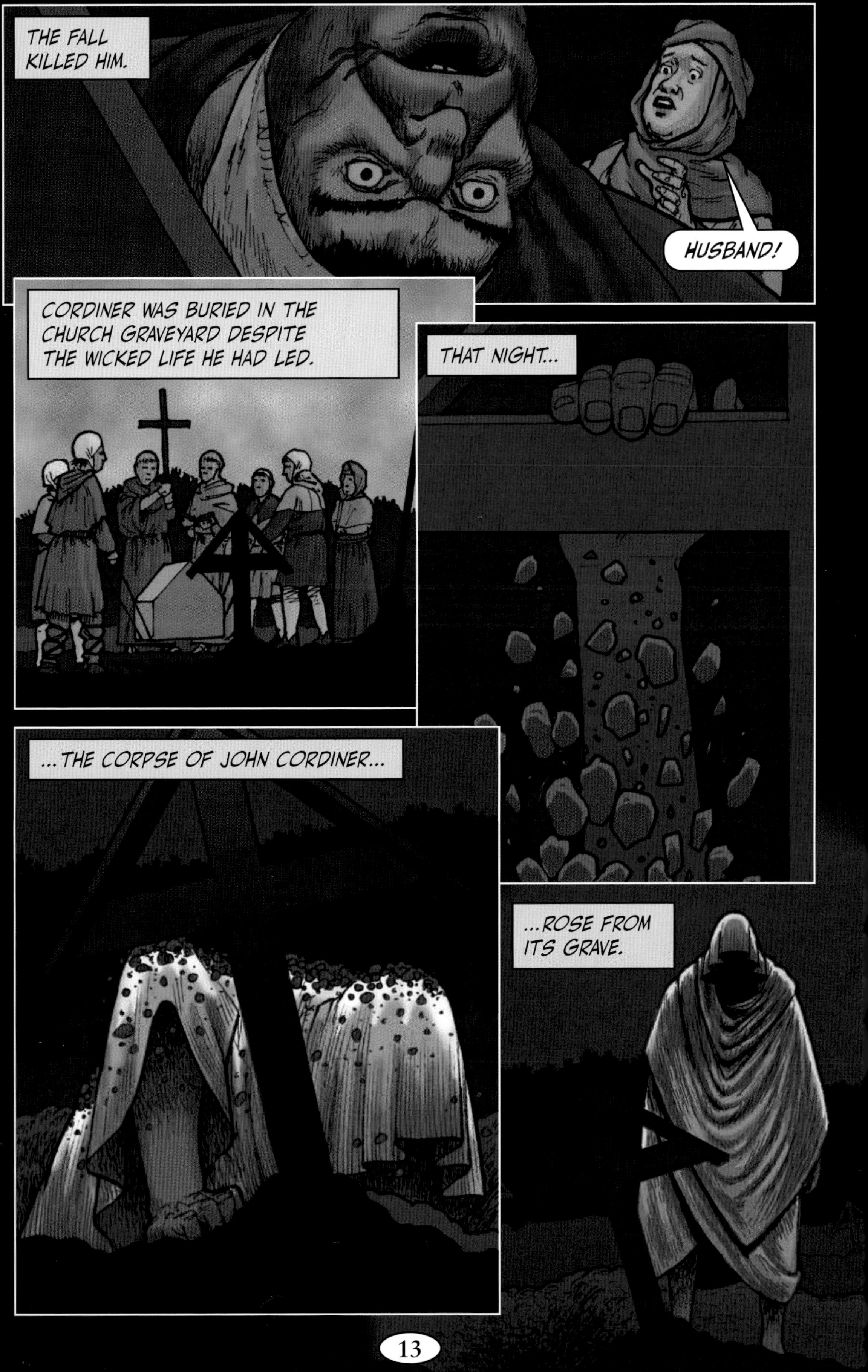
THE FALL KILLED HIM.
HUSBAND!
CORDINER WAS BURIED IN THE CHURCH GRAVEYARD DESPITE THE WICKED LIFE HE HAD LED.
THAT NIGHT...
...THE CORPSE OF JOHN CORDINER...
...ROSE FROM ITS GRAVE.

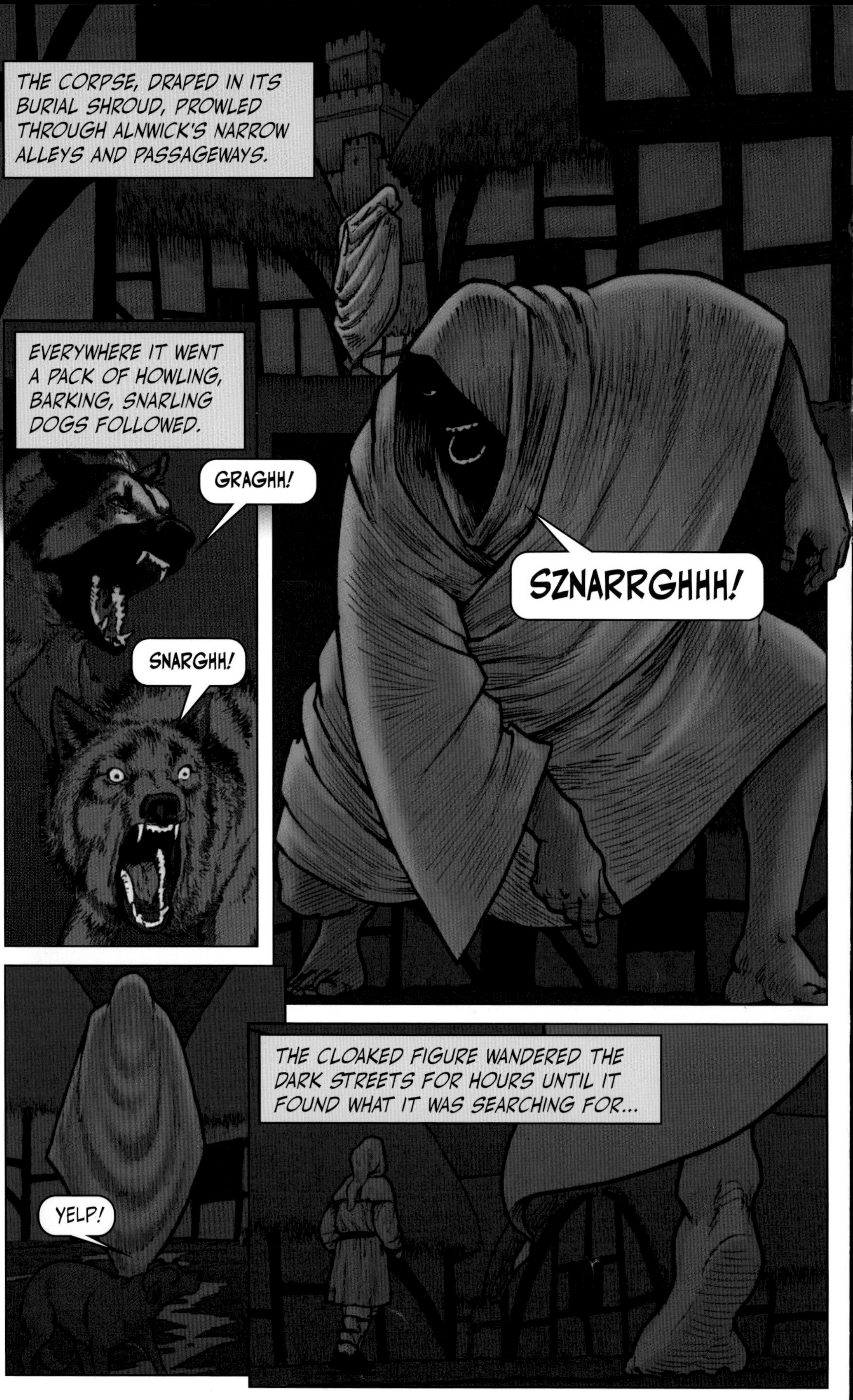
THE CORPSE, DRAPED IN ITS BURIAL SHROUD, PROWLED THROUGH ALNWICK'S NARROW ALLEYS AND PASSAGEWAYS.
EVERYWHERE IT WENT A PACK OF HOWLING, BARKING, SNARLING DOGS FOLLOWED.
GRAGHH!
SNARGHH!
SZNARRGHHH!
YELP!
THE CLOAKED FIGURE WANDERED THE DARK STREETS FOR HOURS UNTIL IT FOUND WHAT IT WAS SEARCHING FOR...

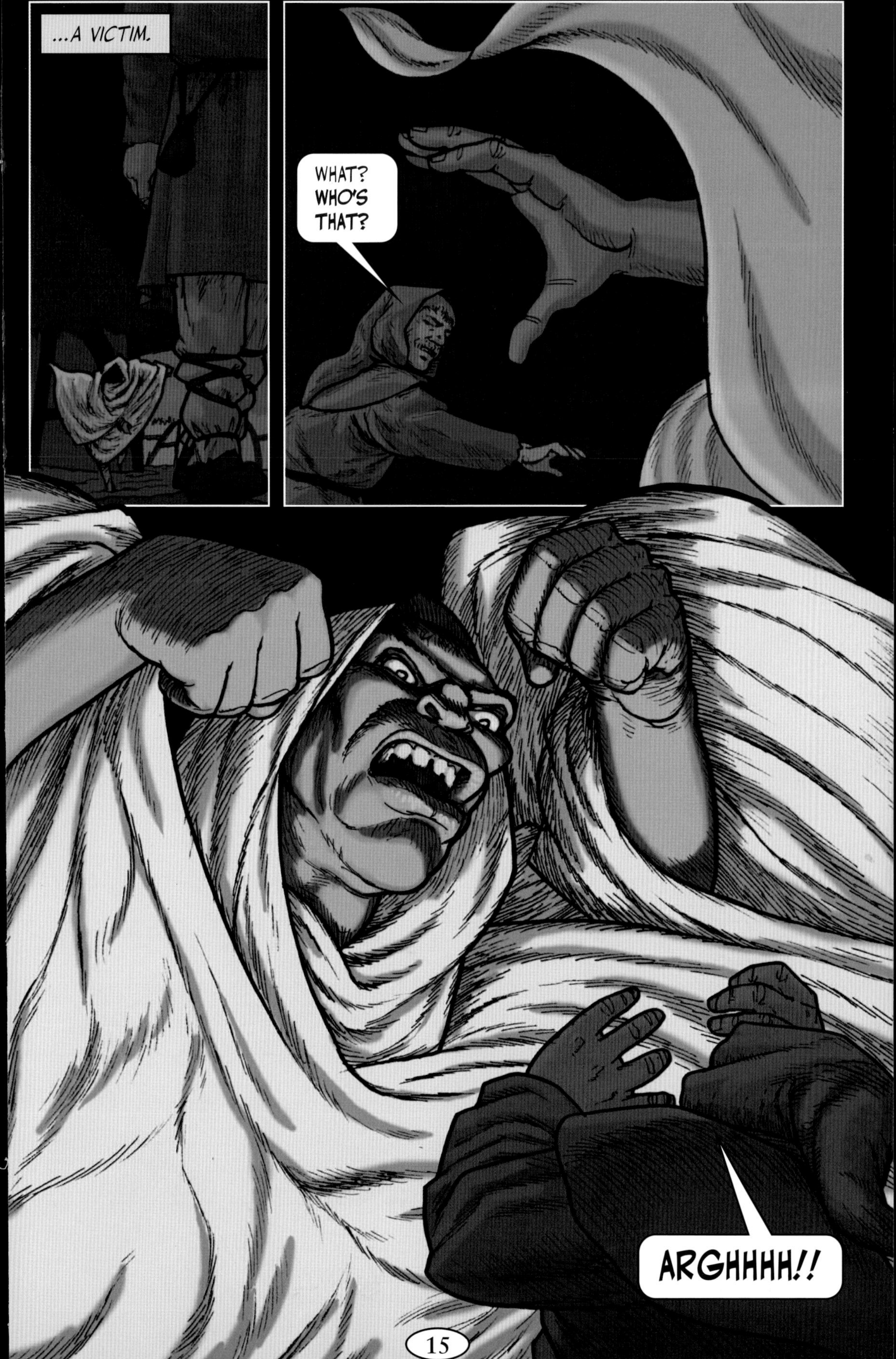
...A VICTIM.
WHAT? WHO'S THAT?
ARGHHHH!!

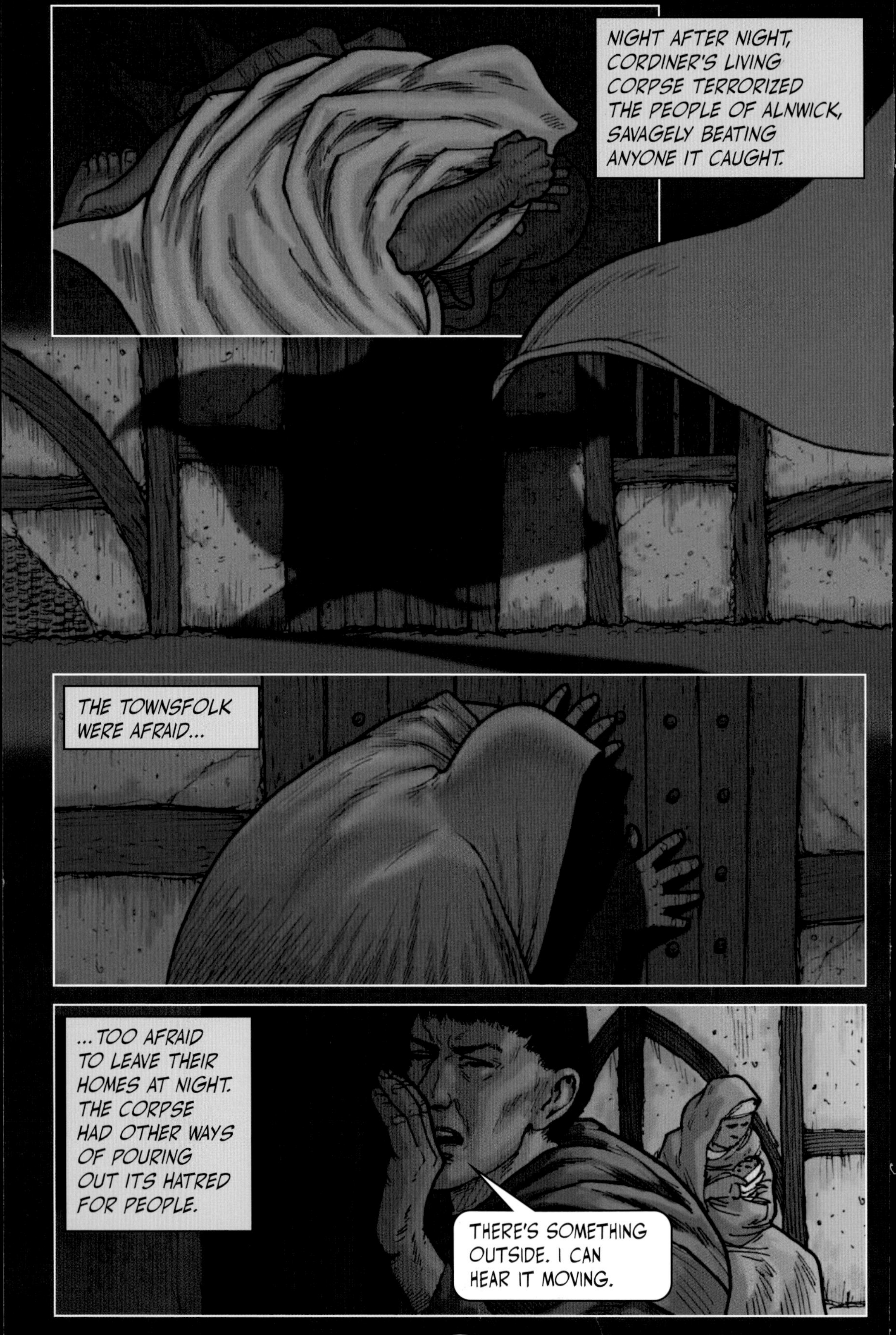
NIGHT AFTER NIGHT, CORDINER'S LIVING CORPSE TERRORIZED THE PEOPLE OF ALNWICK, SAVAGELY BEATING ANYONE IT CAUGHT.
THE TOWNSFOLK WERE AFRAID...
...TOO AFRAID TO LEAVE THEIR HOMES AT NIGHT. THE CORPSE HAD OTHER WAYS OF POURING OUT ITS HATRED FOR PEOPLE.
THERE'S SOMETHING OUTSIDE. I CAN HEAR IT MOVING.

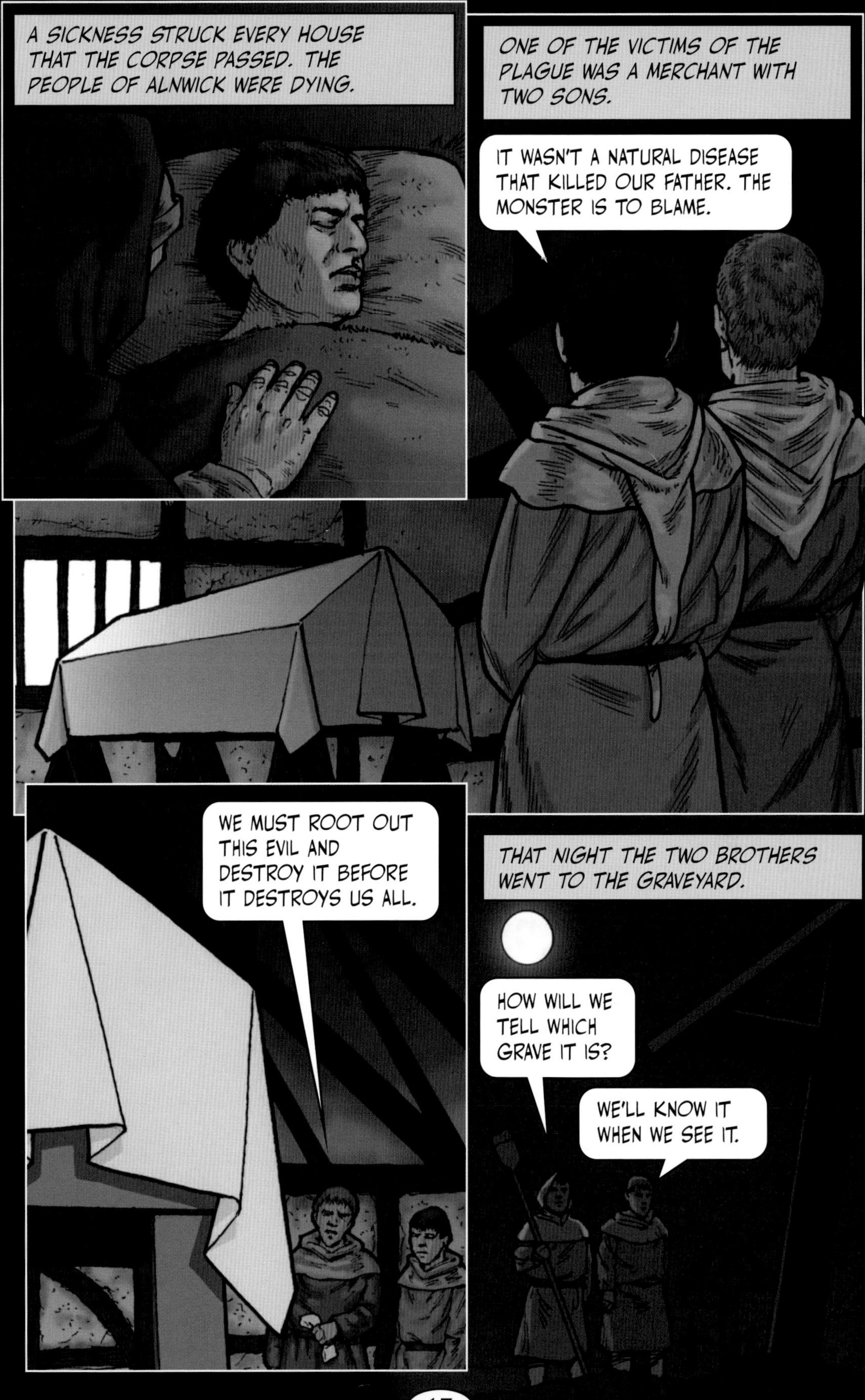
A SICKNESS STRUCK EVERY HOUSE THAT THE CORPSE PASSED. THE PEOPLE OF ALNWICK WERE DYING.
ONE OF THE VICTIMS OF THE PLAGUE WAS A MERCHANT WITH TWO SONS.
IT WASN'T A NATURAL DISEASE THAT KILLED OUR FATHER. THE MONSTER IS TO BLAME.
WE MUST ROOT OUT THIS EVIL AND DESTROY IT BEFORE IT DESTROYS US ALL.
THAT NIGHT THE TWO BROTHERS WENT TO THE GRAVEYARD.
HOW WILL WE TELL WHICH GRAVE IT IS?
WE'LL KNOW IT WHEN WE SEE IT.

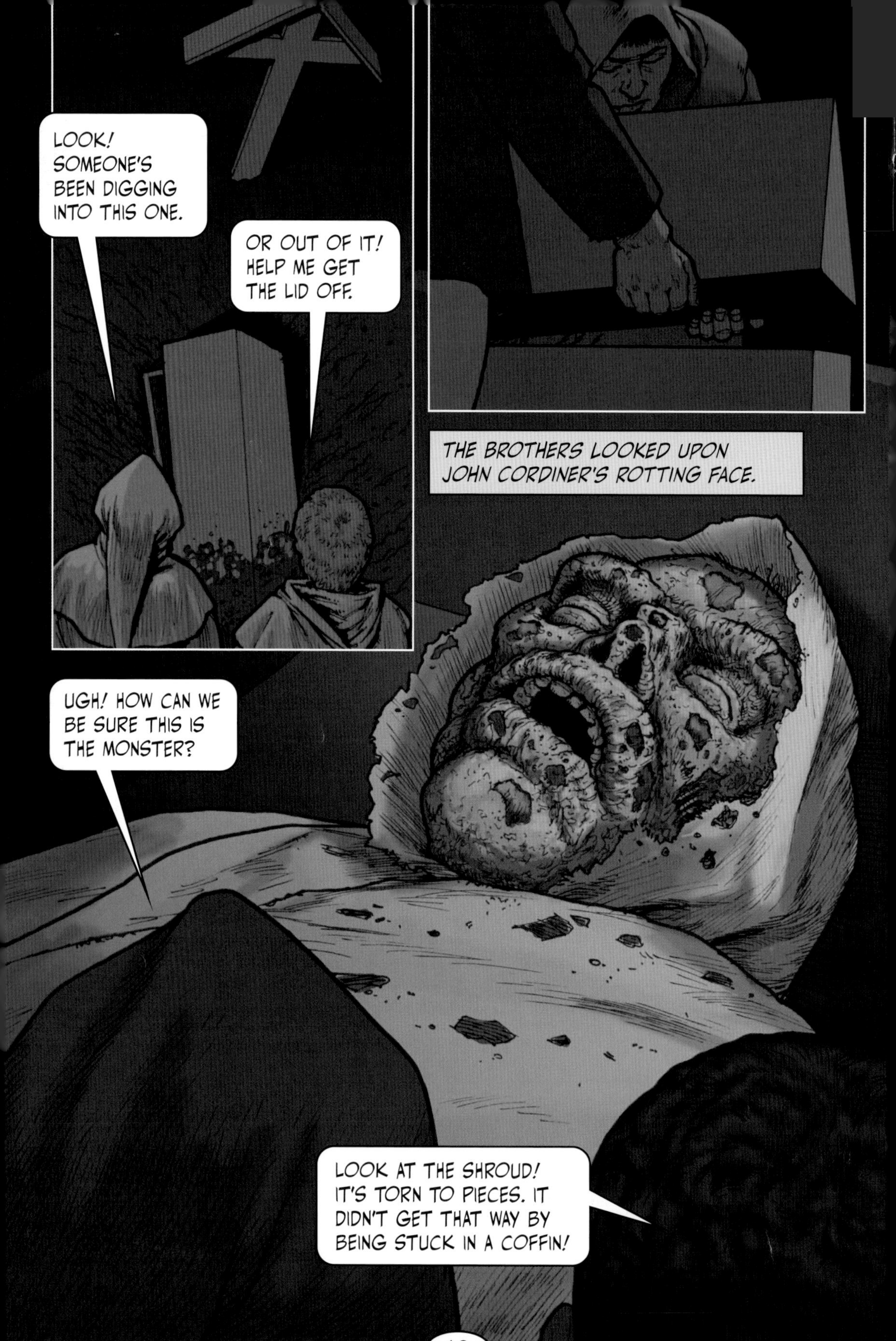
LOOK! SOMEONE'S BEEN DIGGING INTO THIS ONE.
OR OUT OF IT! HELP ME GET THE LID OFF.
THE BROTHERS LOOKED UPON JOHN CORDINER'S ROTTING FACE.
UGH! HOW CAN WE BE SURE THIS IS THE MONSTER?
LOOK AT THE SHROUD! IT'S TORN TO PIECES. IT DIDN'T GET THAT WAY BY BEING STUCK IN A COFFIN!

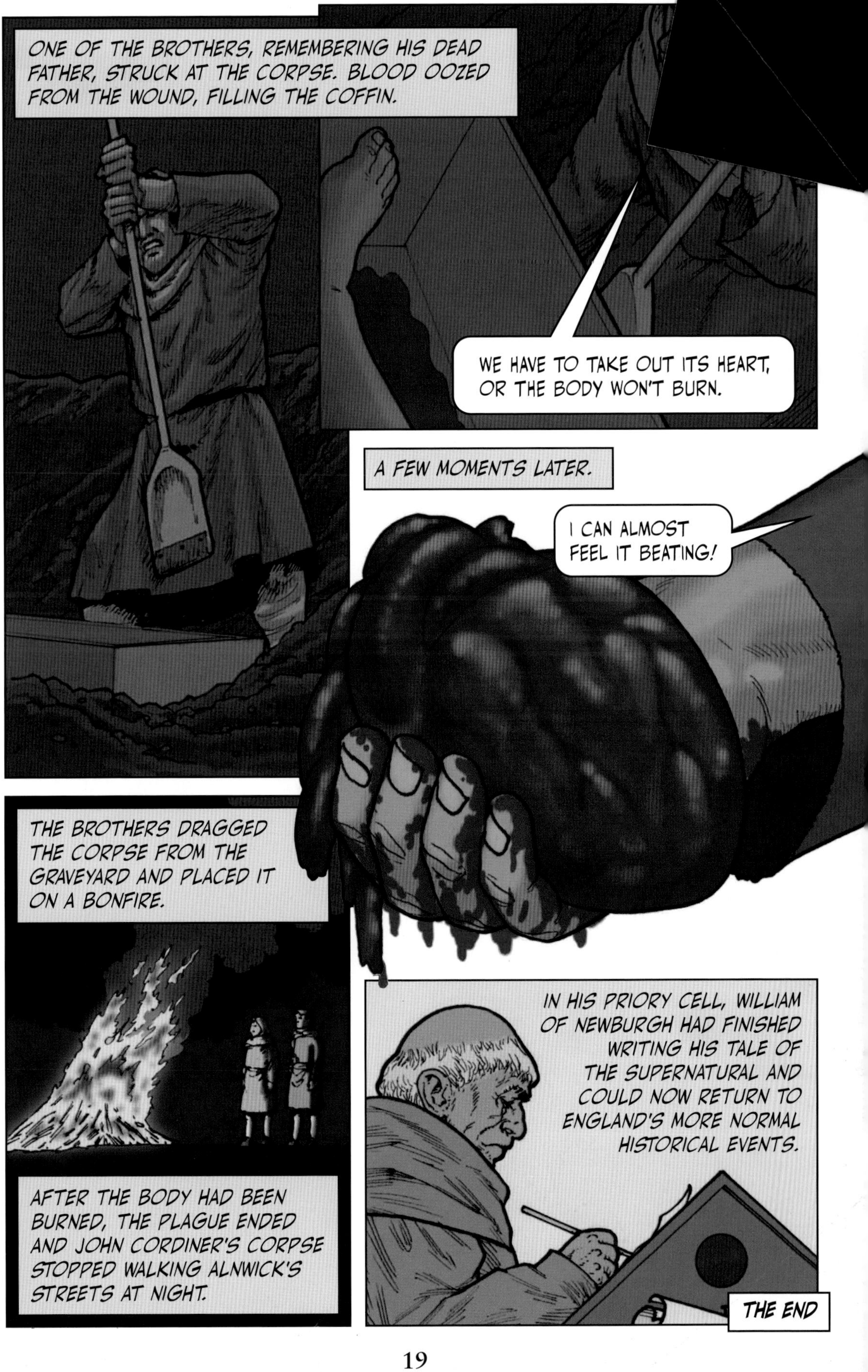
ONE OF THE BROTHERS, REMEMBERING HIS DEAD FATHER, STRUCK AT THE CORPSE. BLOOD OOZED FROM THE WOUND, FILLING THE COFFIN.
WE HAVE TO TAKE OUT ITS HEART, OR THE BODY WON'T BURN.
A FEW MOMENTS LATER.
I CAN ALMOST FEEL IT BEATING!
THE BROTHERS DRAGGED THE CORPSE FROM THE GRAVEYARD AND PLACED IT ON A BONFIRE.
AFTER THE BODY HAD BEEN BURNED, THE PLAGUE ENDED AND JOHN CORDINER'S CORPSE STOPPED WALKING ALNWICK'S STREETS AT NIGHT.
IN HIS PRIORY CELL, WILLIAM OF NEWBURGH HAD FINISHED WRITING HIS TALE OF THE SUPERNATURAL AND COULD NOW RETURN TO ENGLAND'S MORE NORMAL HISTORICAL EVENTS.
THE END

THE HEADLESS HORSEMAN

THE TERROR OF TARRYTOWN, NEW YORK, 1786.

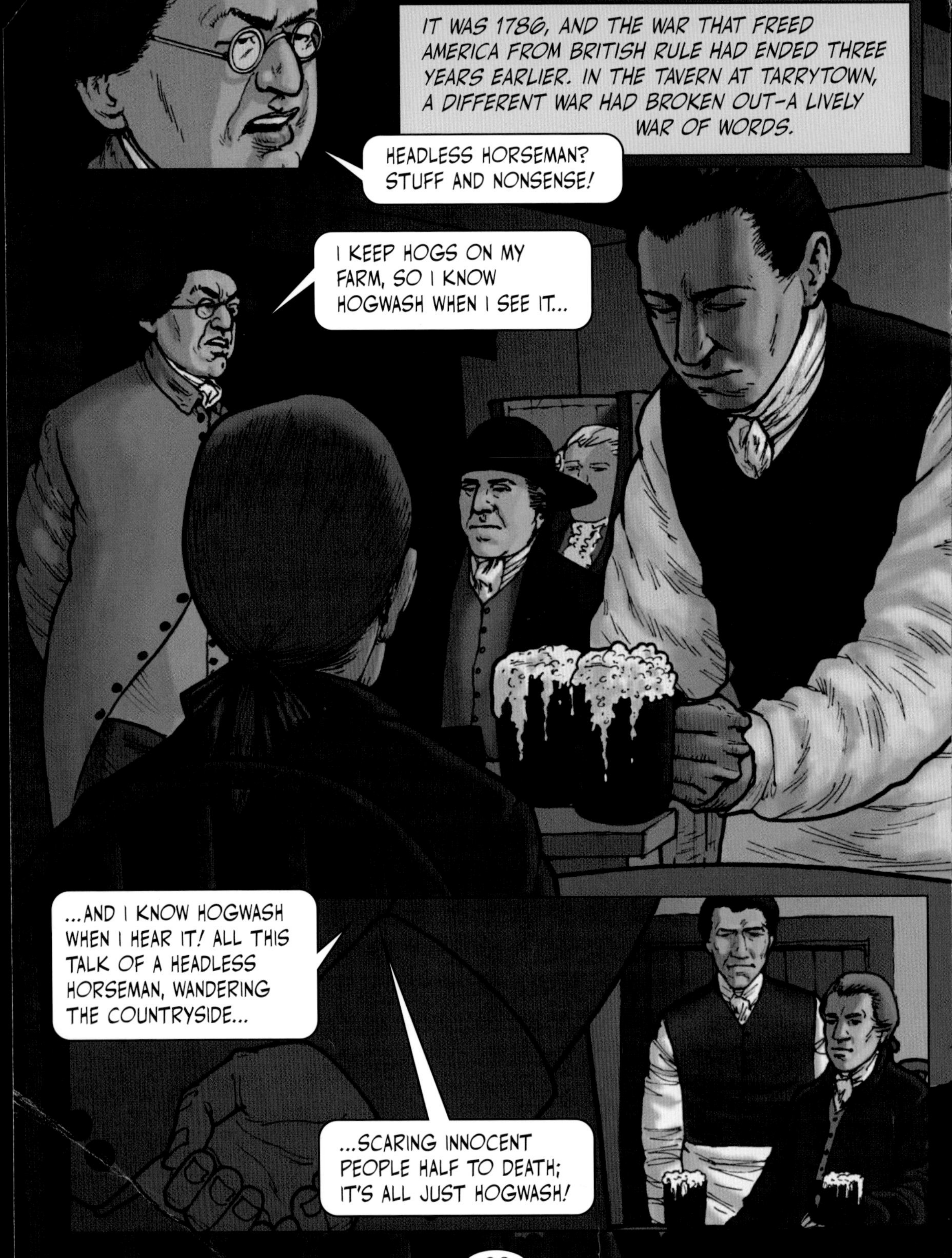
IT WAS 1786, AND THE WAR THAT FREED AMERICA FROM BRITISH RULE HAD ENDED THREE YEARS EARLIER. IN THE TAVERN AT TARRYTOWN, A DIFFERENT WAR HAD BROKEN OUT–A LIVELY WAR OF WORDS.
HEADLESS HORSEMAN? STUFF AND NONSENSE!
I KEEP HOGS ON MY FARM, SO I KNOW HOGWASH WHEN I SEE IT...
...AND I KNOW HOGWASH WHEN I HEAR IT! ALL THIS TALK OF A HEADLESS HORSEMAN, WANDERING THE COUNTRYSIDE...
...SCARING INNOCENT PEOPLE HALF TO DEATH; IT'S ALL JUST HOGWASH!

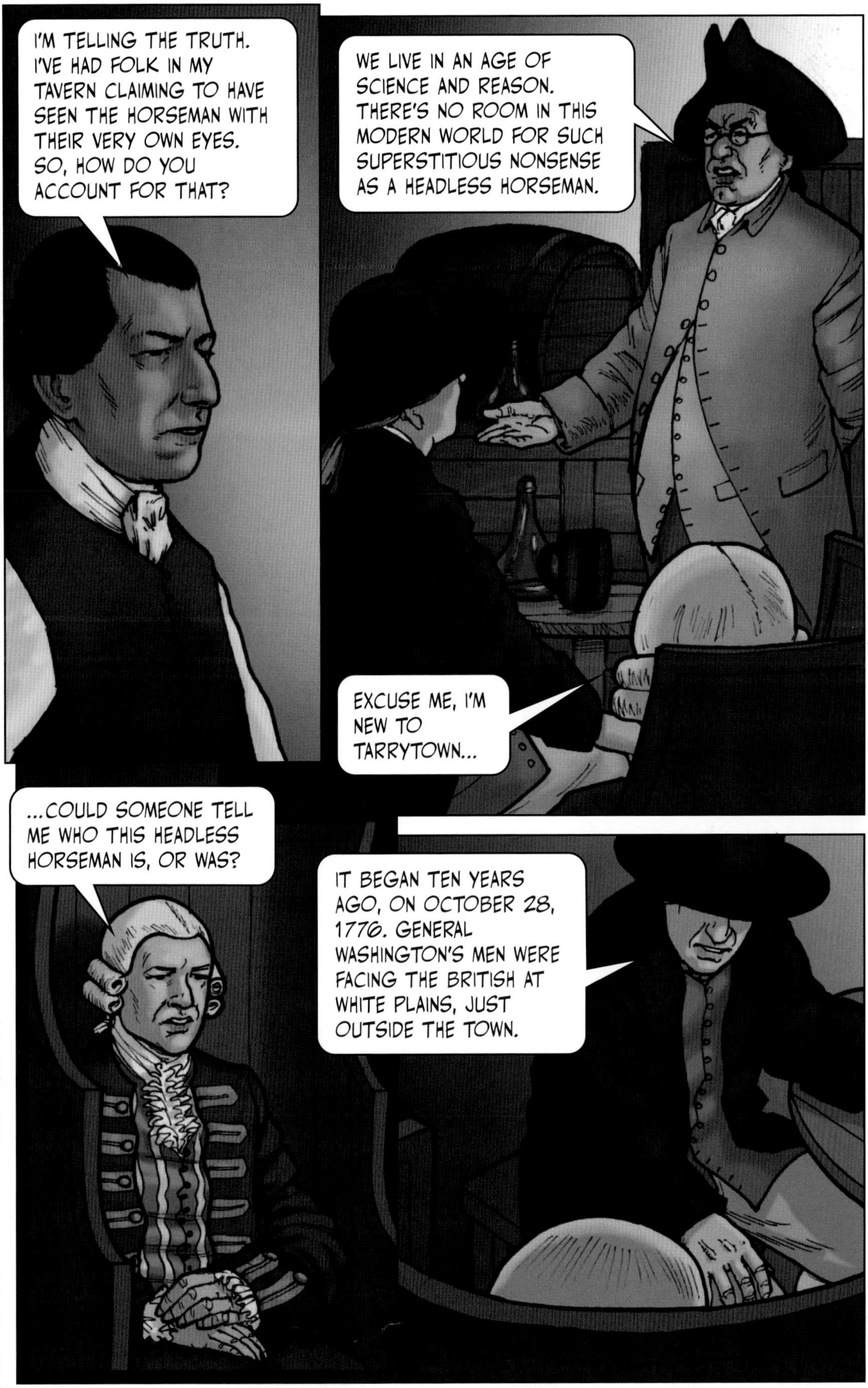
I'M TELLING THE TRUTH. I'VE HAD FOLK IN MY TAVERN CLAIMING TO HAVE SEEN THE HORSEMAN WITH THEIR VERY OWN EYES. SO, HOW DO YOU ACCOUNT FOR THAT?
WE LIVE IN AN AGE OF SCIENCE AND REASON. THERE'S NO ROOM IN THIS MODERN WORLD FOR SUCH SUPERSTITIOUS NONSENSE AS A HEADLESS HORSEMAN.
EXCUSE ME, I'M NEW TO TARRYTOWN...
...COULD SOMEONE TELL ME WHO THIS HEADLESS HORSEMAN IS, OR WAS?
IT BEGAN TEN YEARS AGO, ON OCTOBER 28, 1776. GENERAL WASHINGTON'S MEN WERE FACING THE BRITISH AT WHITE PLAINS, JUST OUTSIDE THE TOWN.

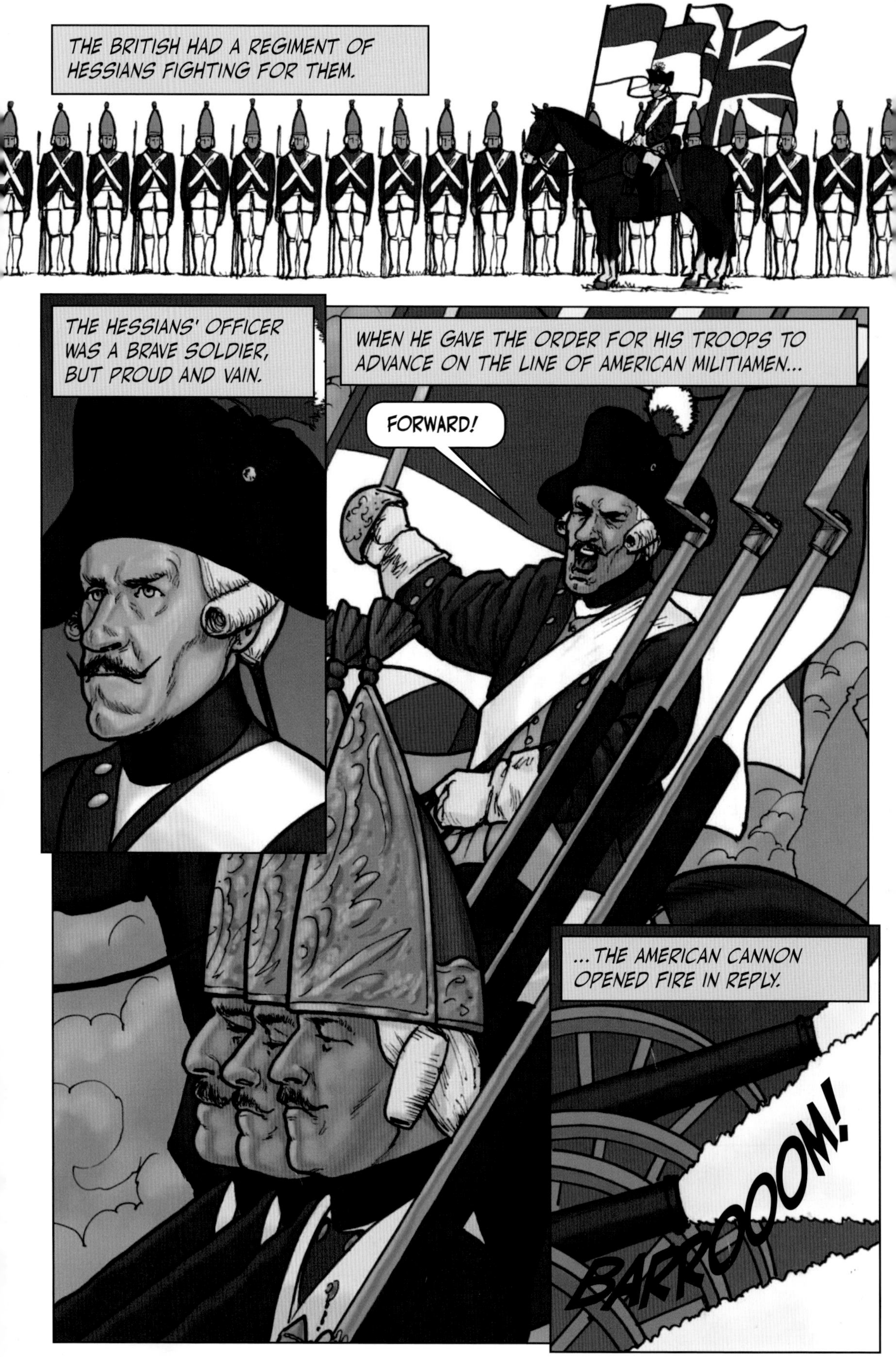
THE BRITISH HAD A REGIMENT OF HESSIANS FIGHTING FOR THEM.
THE HESSIANS' OFFICER WAS A BRAVE SOLDIER, BUT PROUD AND VAIN.
WHEN HE GAVE THE ORDER FOR HIS TROOPS TO ADVANCE ON THE LINE OF AMERICAN MILITIAMEN...
FORWARD!
...THE AMERICAN CANNON OPENED FIRE IN REPLY.
BARROOOM!

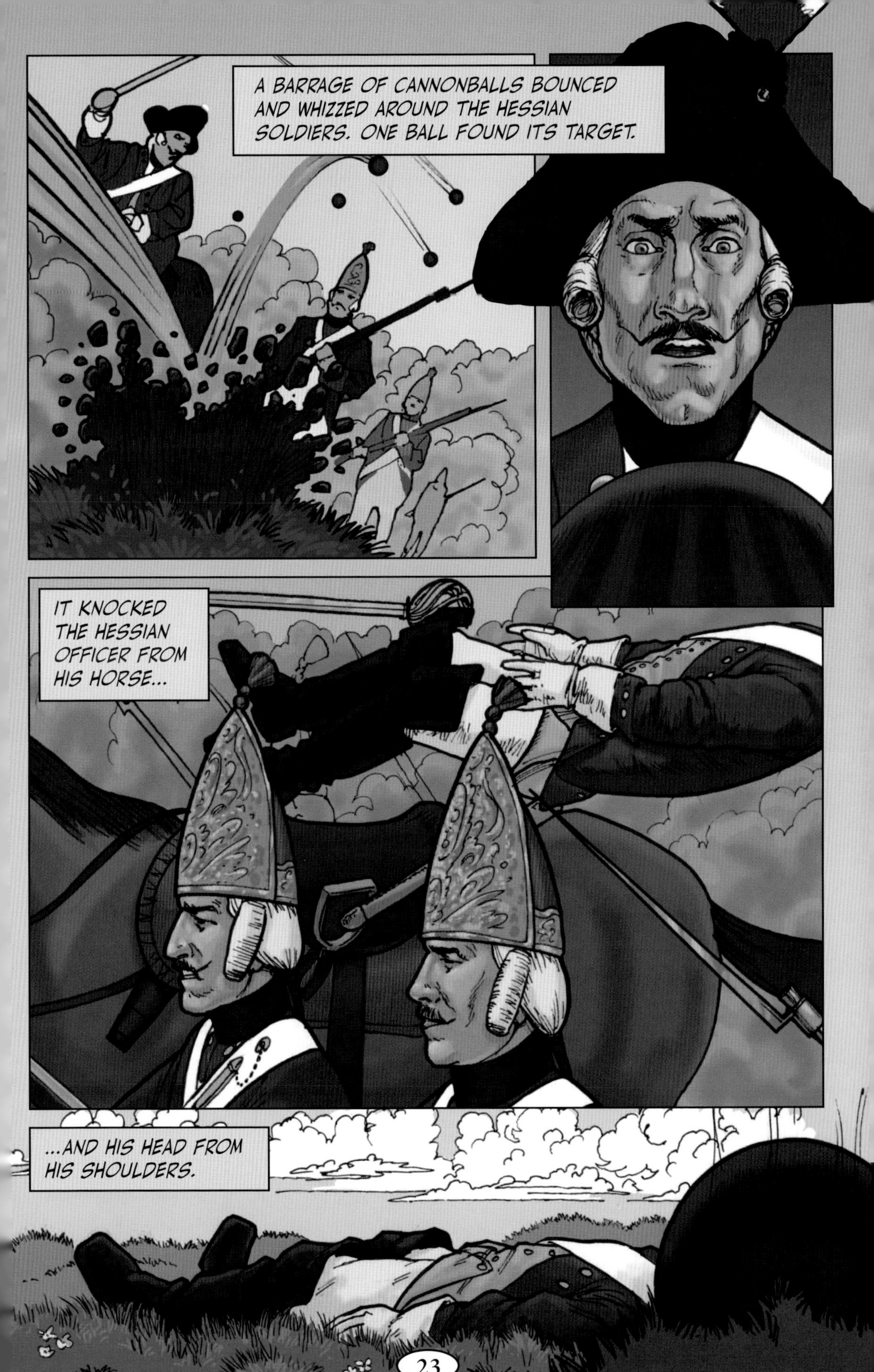
A BARRAGE OF CANNONBALLS BOUNCED AND WHIZZED AROUND THE HESSIAN SOLDIERS. ONE BALL FOUND ITS TARGET.
IT KNOCKED THE HESSIAN OFFICER FROM HIS HORSE...
...AND HIS HEAD FROM HIS SHOULDERS.

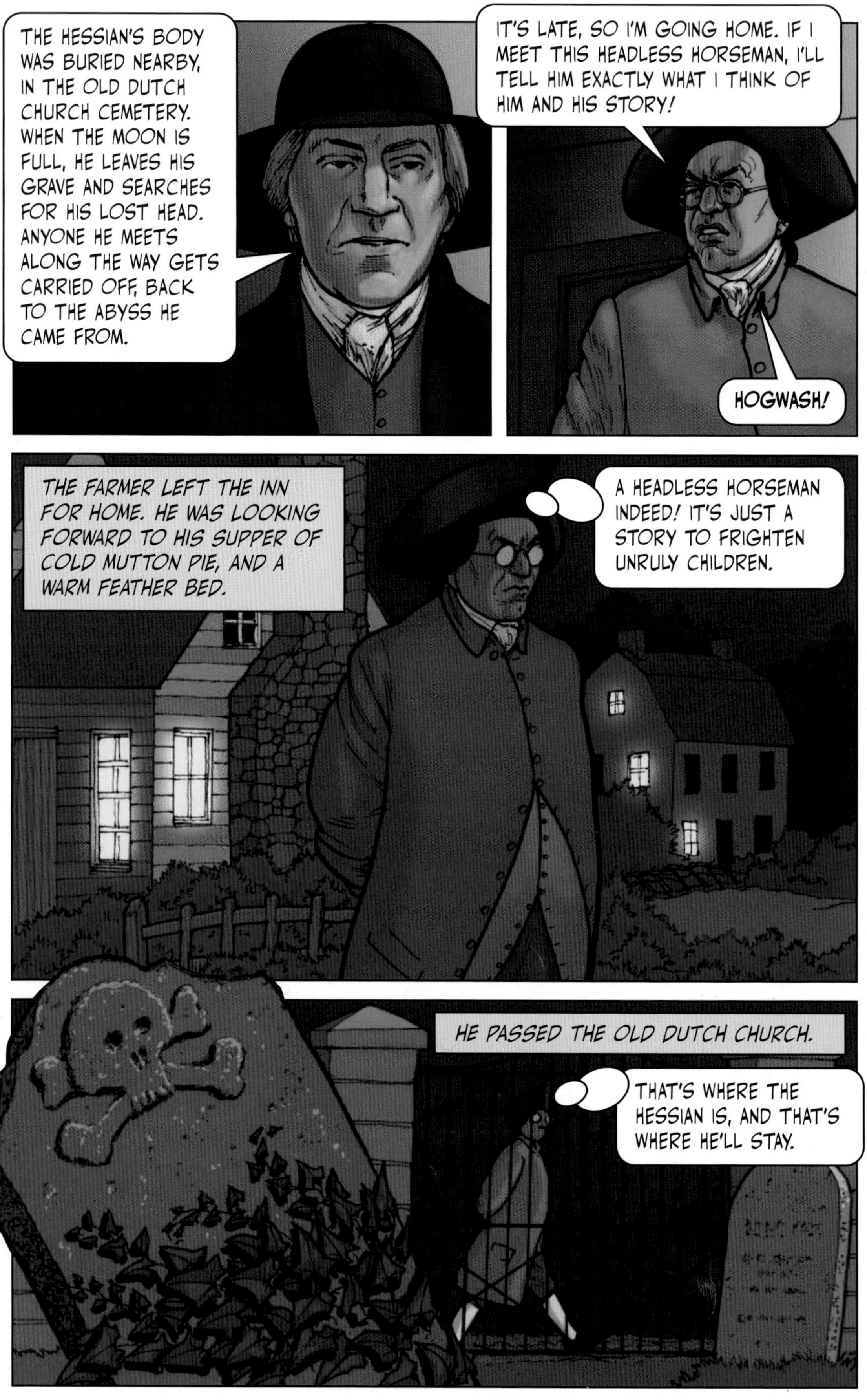
THE HESSIAN'S BODY WAS BURIED NEARBY, IN THE OLD DUTCH CHURCH CEMETERY. WHEN THE MOON IS FULL, HE LEAVES HIS GRAVE AND SEARCHES FOR HIS LOST HEAD. ANYONE HE MEETS ALONG THE WAY GETS CARRIED OFF, BACK TO THE ABYSS HE CAME FROM.
IT'S LATE, SO I'M GOING HOME. IF I MEET THIS HEADLESS HORSEMAN, I'LL TELL HIM EXACTLY WHAT I THINK OF HIM AND HIS STORY!
HOGWASH!
THE FARMER LEFT THE INN FOR HOME. HE WAS LOOKING FORWARD TO HIS SUPPER OF COLD MUTTON PIE, AND A WARM FEATHER BED.
A HEADLESS HORSEMAN INDEED! IT'S JUST A STORY TO FRIGHTEN UNRULY CHILDREN.
HE PASSED THE OLD DUTCH CHURCH.
THAT'S WHERE THE HESSIAN IS, AND THAT'S WHERE HE'LL STAY.

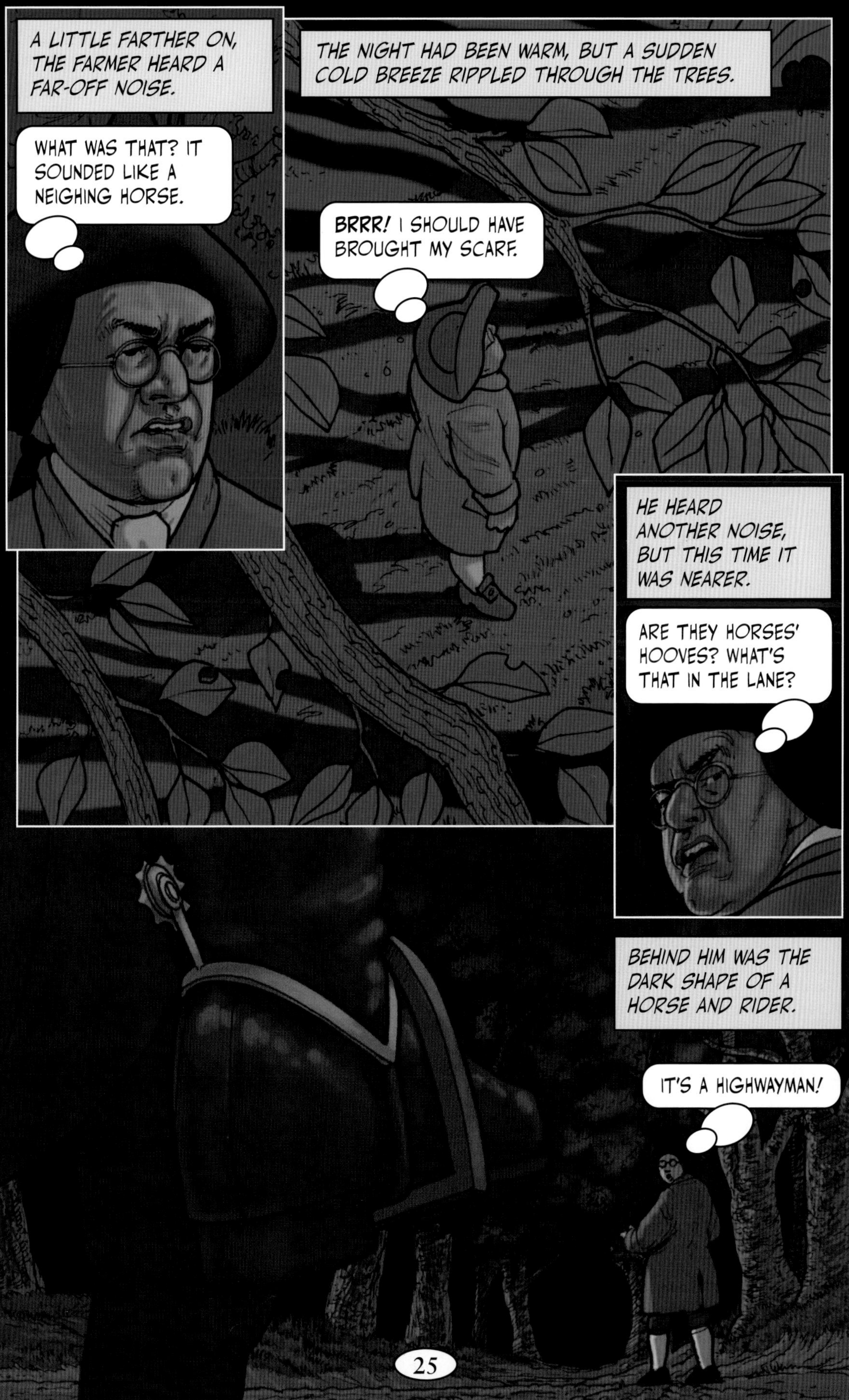
A LITTLE FARTHER ON, THE FARMER HEARD A FAR-OFF NOISE.
WHAT WAS THAT? IT SOUNDED LIKE A NEIGHING HORSE.
THE NIGHT HAD BEEN WARM, BUT A SUDDEN COLD BREEZE RIPPLED THROUGH THE TREES.
BRRR! I SHOULD HAVE BROUGHT MY SCARF.
HE HEARD ANOTHER NOISE, BUT THIS TIME IT WAS NEARER.
ARE THEY HORSES' HOOVES? WHAT'S THAT IN THE LANE?
BEHIND HIM WAS THE DARK SHAPE OF A HORSE AND RIDER.
IT'S A HIGHWAYMAN!

SUDDENLY, THE RIDER DUG IN HIS SPURS AND THE HORSE BOUNDED FORWARD. THE FARMER TURNED...

HELP! HELP ME, SOMEONE! MURDER!

...AND RAN FOR HIS LIFE.

BUT THE RIDER QUICKLY CAUGHT UP WITH HIM.

UH?

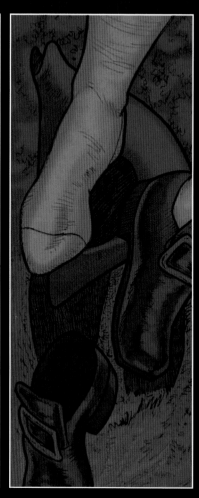

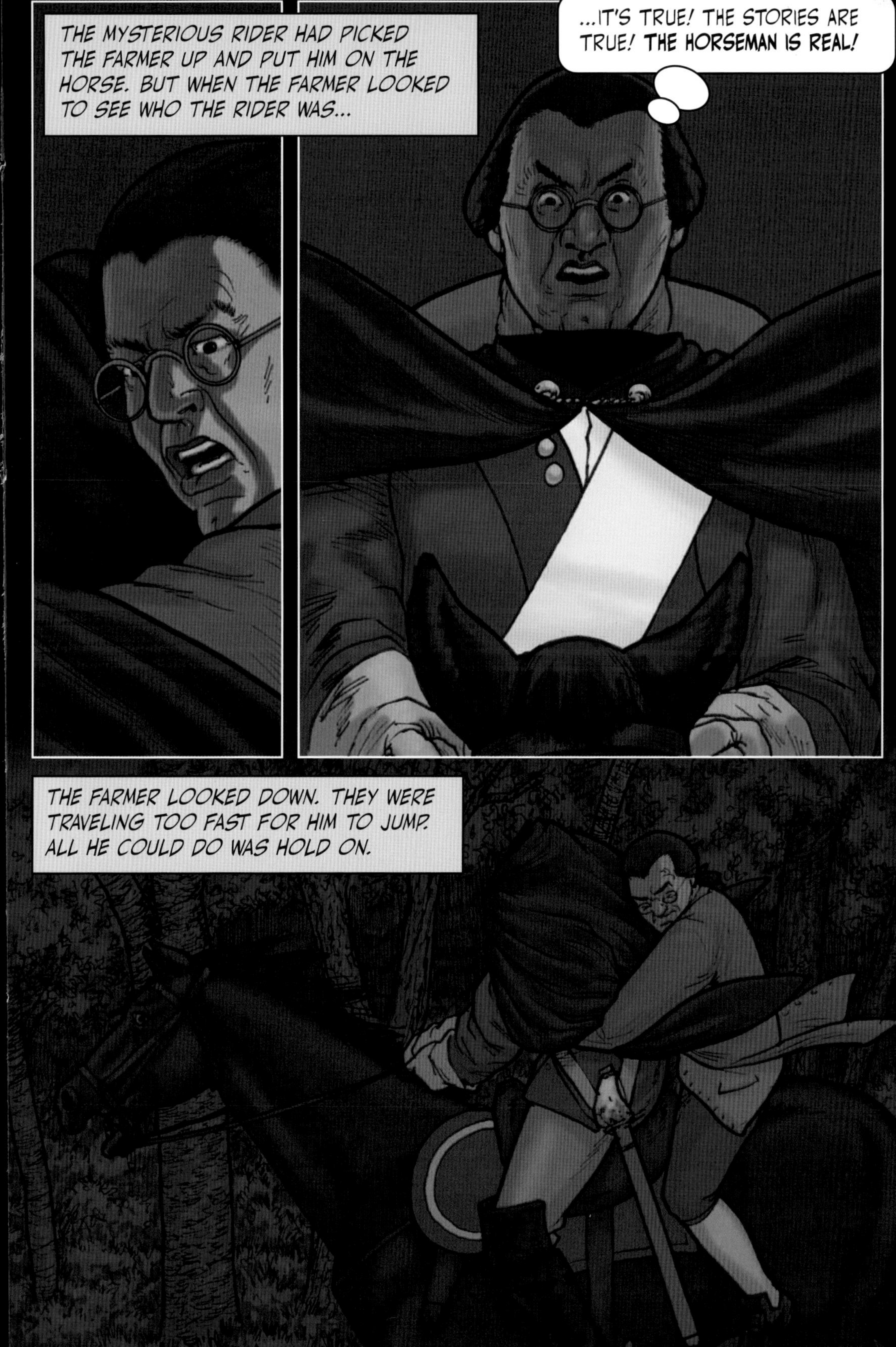
THE MYSTERIOUS RIDER HAD PICKED THE FARMER UP AND PUT HIM ON THE HORSE. BUT WHEN THE FARMER LOOKED TO SEE WHO THE RIDER WAS...
...IT'S TRUE! THE STORIES ARE TRUE! THE HORSEMAN IS REAL!
THE FARMER LOOKED DOWN. THEY WERE TRAVELING TOO FAST FOR HIM TO JUMP. ALL HE COULD DO WAS HOLD ON.

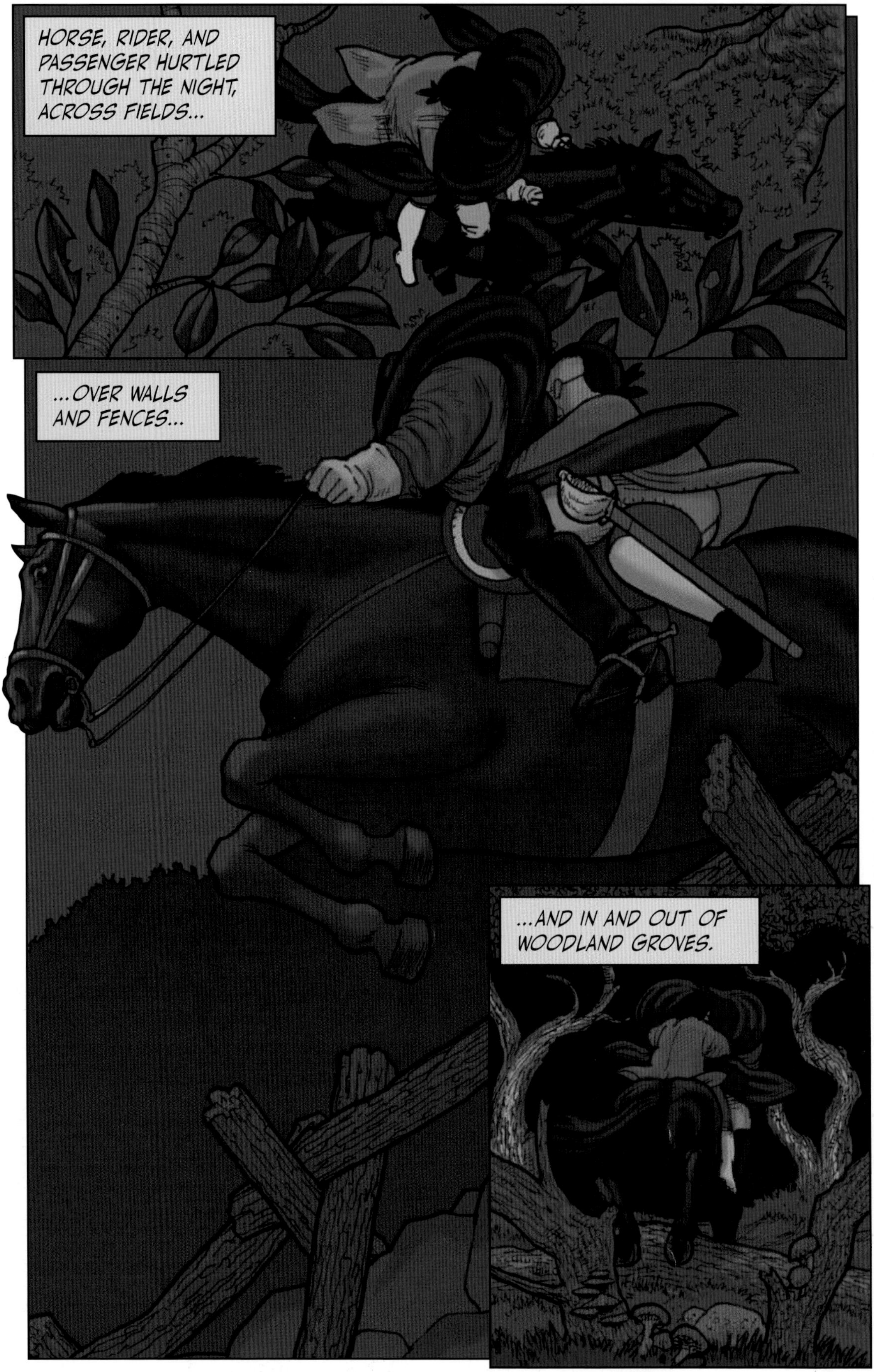
HORSE, RIDER, AND PASSENGER HURTLED THROUGH THE NIGHT, ACROSS FIELDS...
...OVER WALLS AND FENCES...
...AND IN AND OUT OF WOODLAND GROVES.

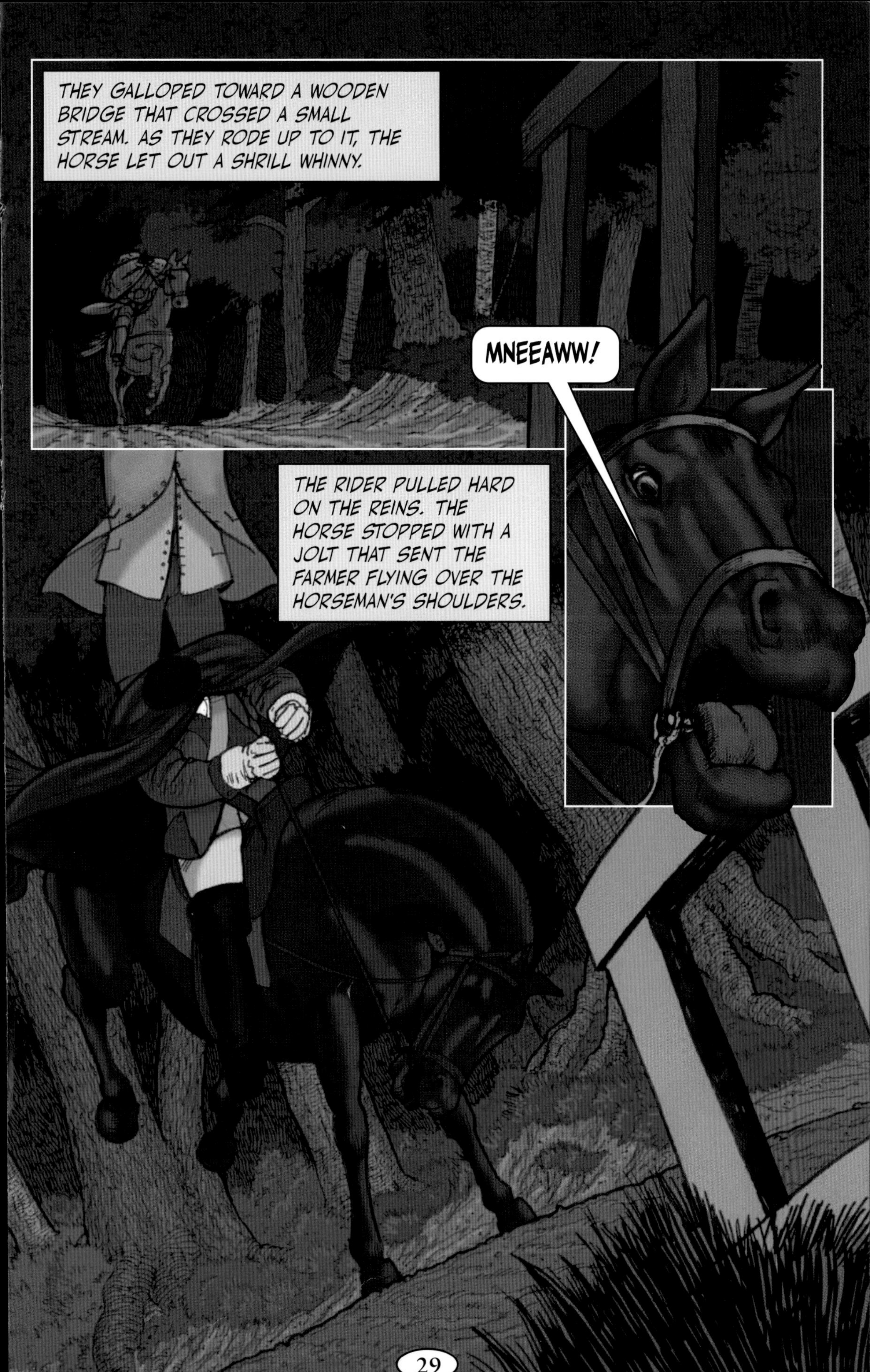
THEY GALLOPED TOWARD A WOODEN BRIDGE THAT CROSSED A SMALL STREAM. AS THEY RODE UP TO IT, THE HORSE LET OUT A SHRILL WHINNY.
MNEEAWW!
THE RIDER PULLED HARD ON THE REINS. THE HORSE STOPPED WITH A JOLT THAT SENT THE FARMER FLYING OVER THE HORSEMAN'S SHOULDERS.

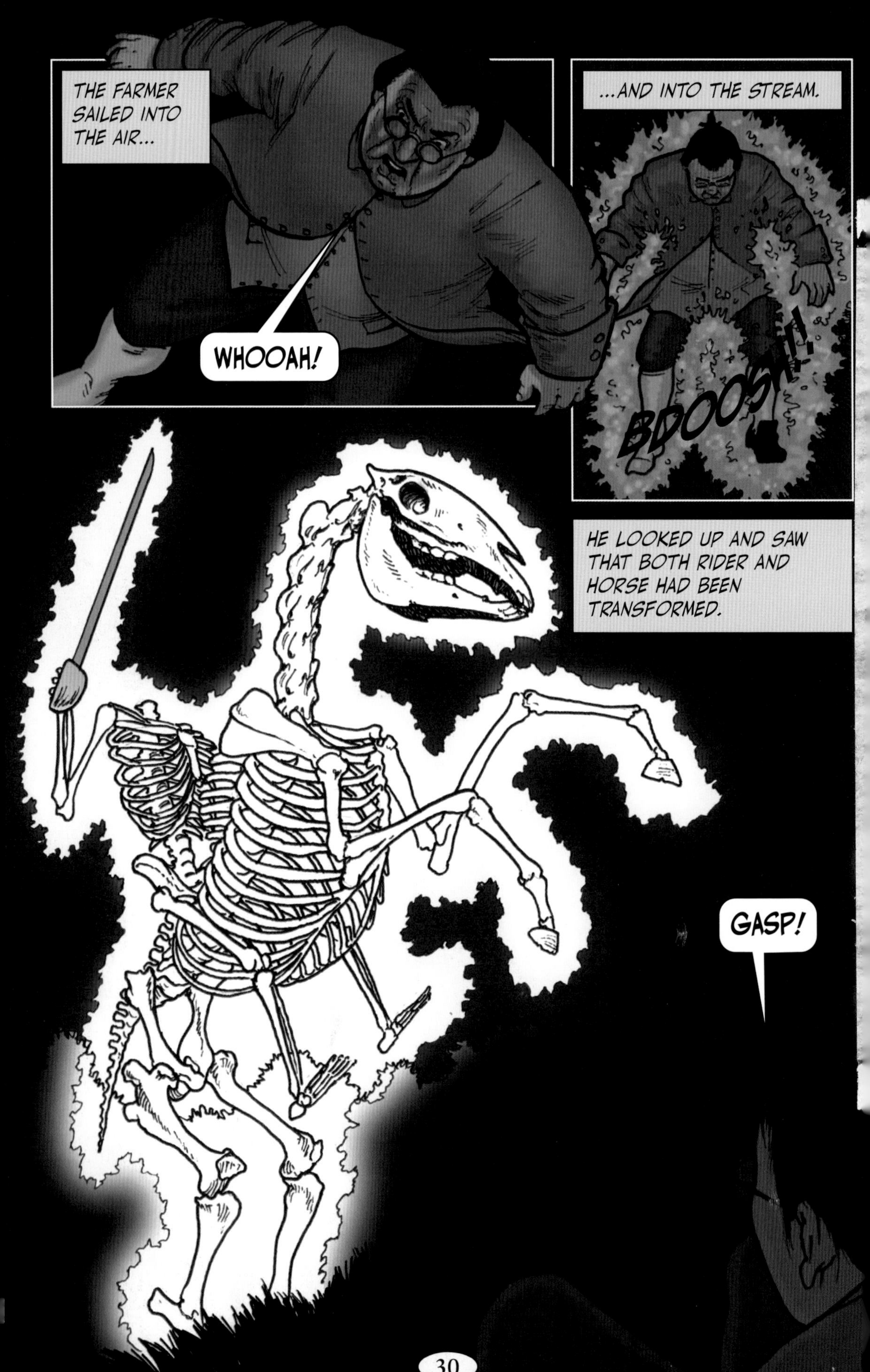
THE FARMER SAILED INTO THE AIR...
WHOOAH!
...AND INTO THE STREAM.
BDOOSH!!
HE LOOKED UP AND SAW THAT BOTH RIDER AND HORSE HAD BEEN TRANSFORMED.
GASP!

BEFORE THE FARMER HAD TIME TO MOVE, THE HORSEMAN TURNED HIS SKELETAL HORSE AND RODE AWAY.

THEY DID NOT GO FAR. WITH A DEAFENING CLAP OF THUNDER, A CREVICE OPENED UP IN THE GROUND.

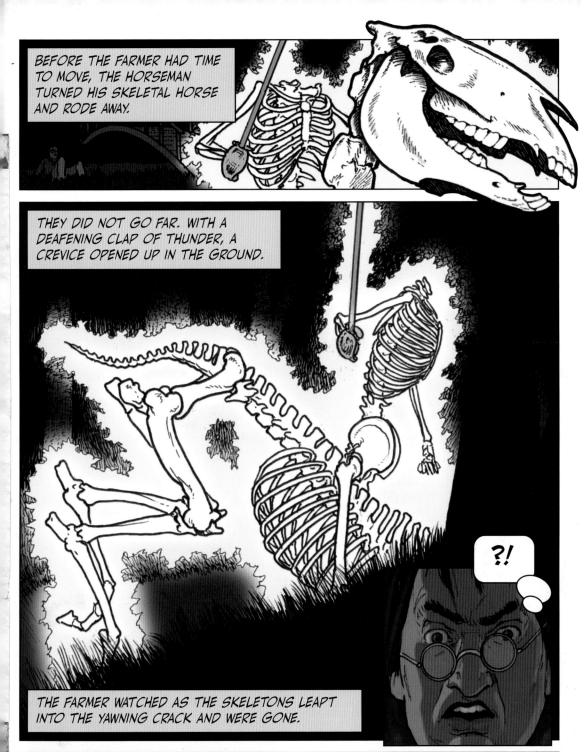

?!

THE FARMER WATCHED AS THE SKELETONS LEAPT INTO THE YAWNING CRACK AND WERE GONE.

THE FARMER TRUDGED HOME, TIRED, SORE, AND WET. THE STREAM THAT DRENCHED HIM HAD ALSO SAVED HIM; THE HEADLESS HORSEMAN COULD NOT CROSS RUNNING WATER. IN THE FUTURE, WHENEVER THE TALK TURNED TO THE SUBJECT OF THE HESSIAN, HE KEPT HIS MOUTH FIRMLY SHUT.

THE END

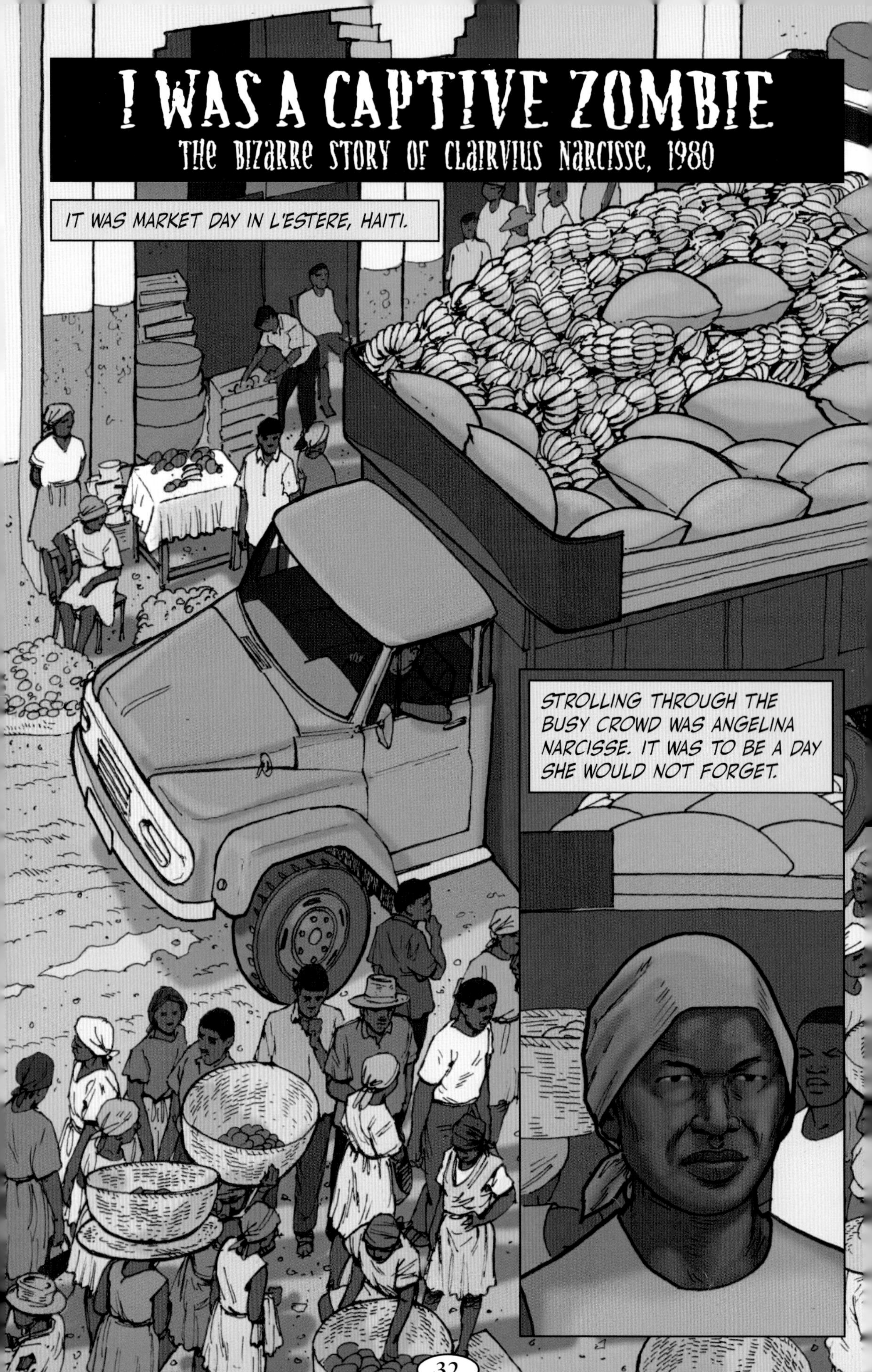
I WAS A CAPTIVE ZOMBIE
THE BIZARRE STORY OF CLAIRVIUS NARCISSE, 1980
IT WAS MARKET DAY IN L'ESTERE, HAITI.
STROLLING THROUGH THE BUSY CROWD WAS ANGELINA NARCISSE. IT WAS TO BE A DAY SHE WOULD NOT FORGET.

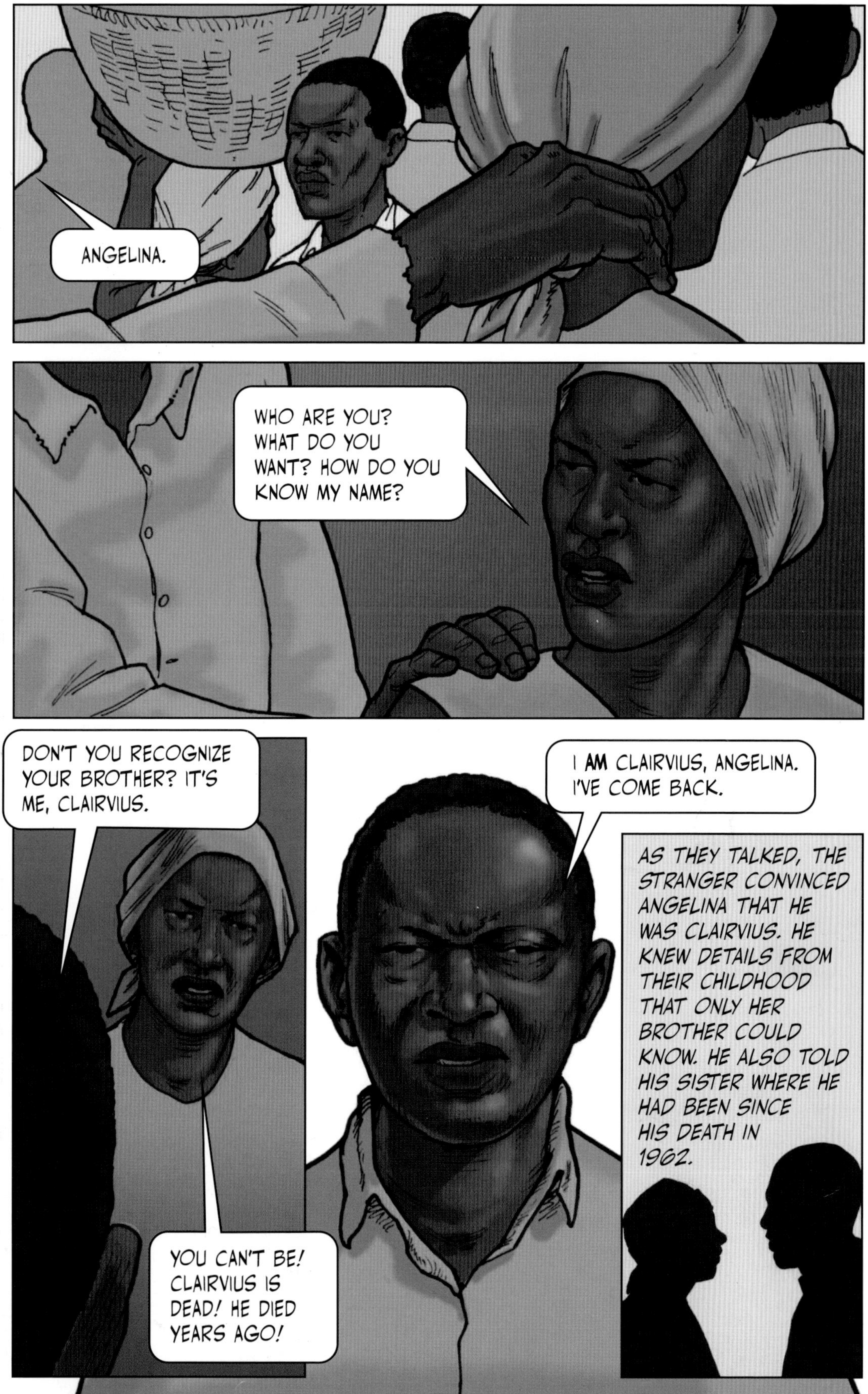
ANGELINA.
WHO ARE YOU? WHAT DO YOU WANT? HOW DO YOU KNOW MY NAME?
DON'T YOU RECOGNIZE YOUR BROTHER? IT'S ME, CLAIRVIUS.
YOU CAN'T BE! CLAIRVIUS IS DEAD! HE DIED YEARS AGO!
I **AM** CLAIRVIUS, ANGELINA. I'VE COME BACK.
AS THEY TALKED, THE STRANGER CONVINCED ANGELINA THAT HE WAS CLAIRVIUS. HE KNEW DETAILS FROM THEIR CHILDHOOD THAT ONLY HER BROTHER COULD KNOW. HE ALSO TOLD HIS SISTER WHERE HE HAD BEEN SINCE HIS DEATH IN 1962.

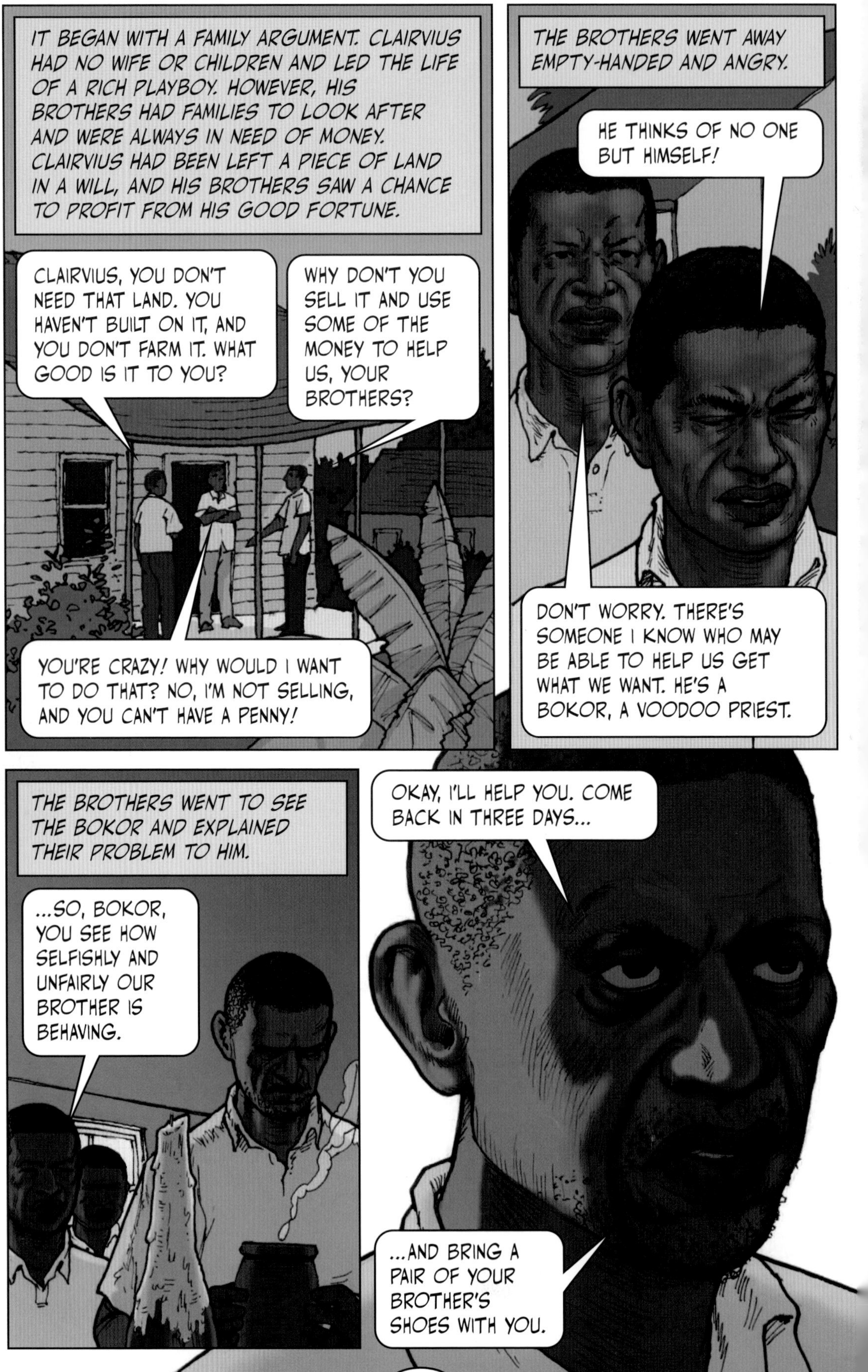
IT BEGAN WITH A FAMILY ARGUMENT. CLAIRVIUS HAD NO WIFE OR CHILDREN AND LED THE LIFE OF A RICH PLAYBOY. HOWEVER, HIS BROTHERS HAD FAMILIES TO LOOK AFTER AND WERE ALWAYS IN NEED OF MONEY. CLAIRVIUS HAD BEEN LEFT A PIECE OF LAND IN A WILL, AND HIS BROTHERS SAW A CHANCE TO PROFIT FROM HIS GOOD FORTUNE.
CLAIRVIUS, YOU DON'T NEED THAT LAND. YOU HAVEN'T BUILT ON IT, AND YOU DON'T FARM IT. WHAT GOOD IS IT TO YOU?
WHY DON'T YOU SELL IT AND USE SOME OF THE MONEY TO HELP US, YOUR BROTHERS?
YOU'RE CRAZY! WHY WOULD I WANT TO DO THAT? NO, I'M NOT SELLING, AND YOU CAN'T HAVE A PENNY!
THE BROTHERS WENT AWAY EMPTY-HANDED AND ANGRY.
HE THINKS OF NO ONE BUT HIMSELF!
DON'T WORRY. THERE'S SOMEONE I KNOW WHO MAY BE ABLE TO HELP US GET WHAT WE WANT. HE'S A BOKOR, A VOODOO PRIEST.
THE BROTHERS WENT TO SEE THE BOKOR AND EXPLAINED THEIR PROBLEM TO HIM.
...SO, BOKOR, YOU SEE HOW SELFISHLY AND UNFAIRLY OUR BROTHER IS BEHAVING.
OKAY, I'LL HELP YOU. COME BACK IN THREE DAYS...
...AND BRING A PAIR OF YOUR BROTHER'S SHOES WITH YOU.

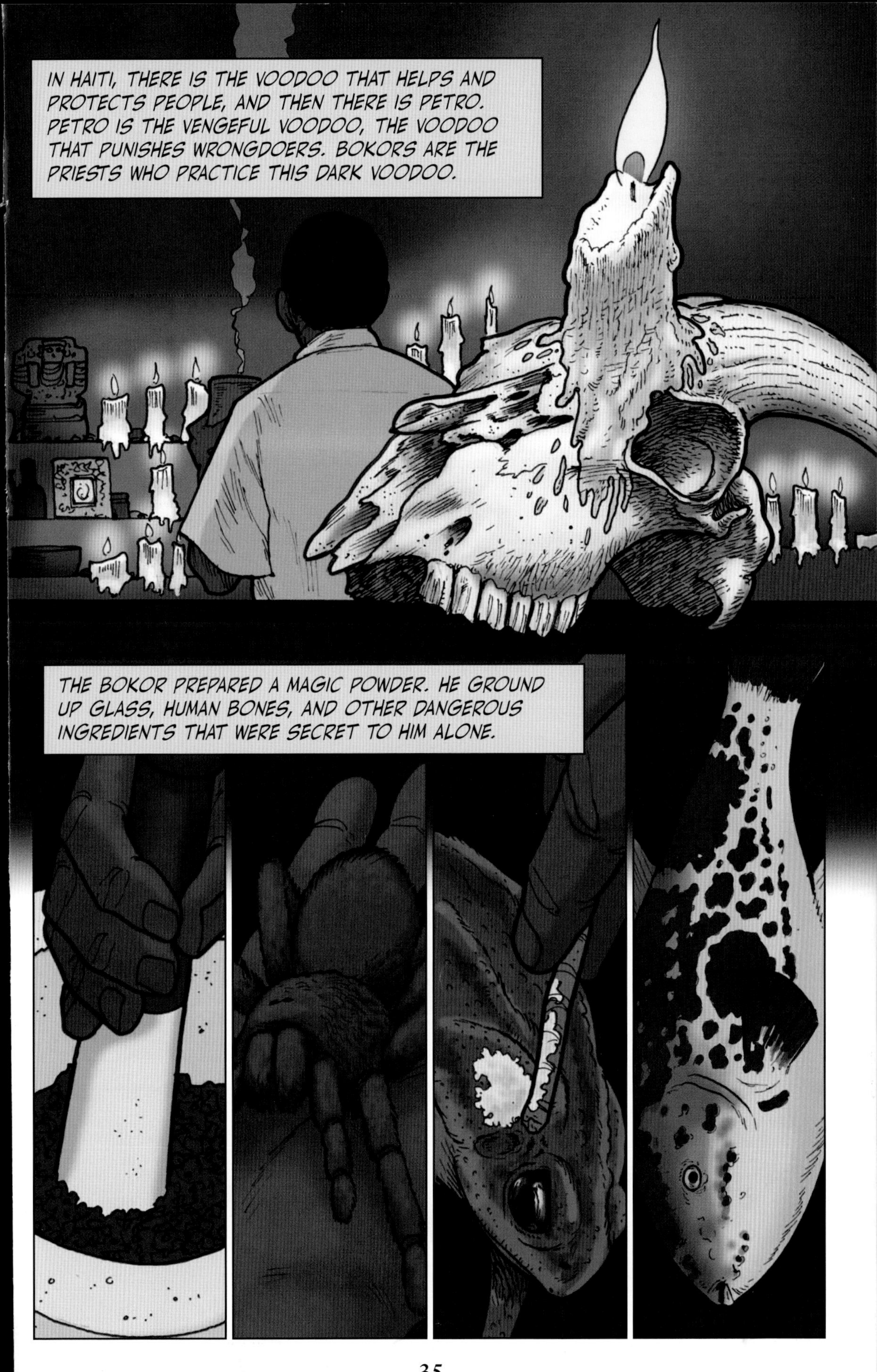
IN HAITI, THERE IS THE VOODOO THAT HELPS AND PROTECTS PEOPLE, AND THEN THERE IS PETRO. PETRO IS THE VENGEFUL VOODOO, THE VOODOO THAT PUNISHES WRONGDOERS. BOKORS ARE THE PRIESTS WHO PRACTICE THIS DARK VOODOO.
THE BOKOR PREPARED A MAGIC POWDER. HE GROUND UP GLASS, HUMAN BONES, AND OTHER DANGEROUS INGREDIENTS THAT WERE SECRET TO HIM ALONE.

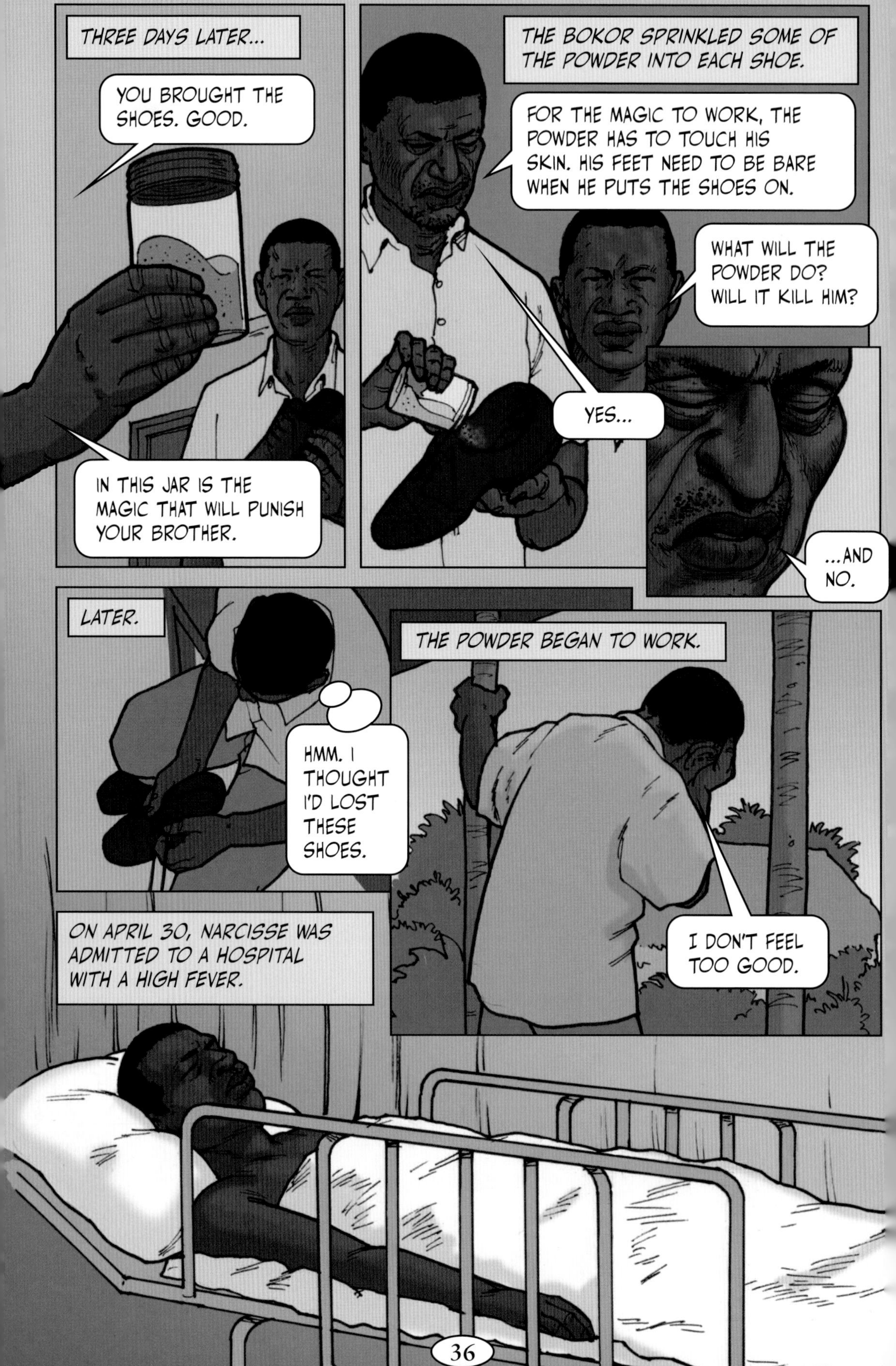
THREE DAYS LATER...
YOU BROUGHT THE SHOES. GOOD.
IN THIS JAR IS THE MAGIC THAT WILL PUNISH YOUR BROTHER.
THE BOKOR SPRINKLED SOME OF THE POWDER INTO EACH SHOE.
FOR THE MAGIC TO WORK, THE POWDER HAS TO TOUCH HIS SKIN. HIS FEET NEED TO BE BARE WHEN HE PUTS THE SHOES ON.
WHAT WILL THE POWDER DO? WILL IT KILL HIM?
YES...
...AND NO.
LATER.
HMM. I THOUGHT I'D LOST THESE SHOES.
THE POWDER BEGAN TO WORK.
I DON'T FEEL TOO GOOD.
ON APRIL 30, NARCISSE WAS ADMITTED TO A HOSPITAL WITH A HIGH FEVER.

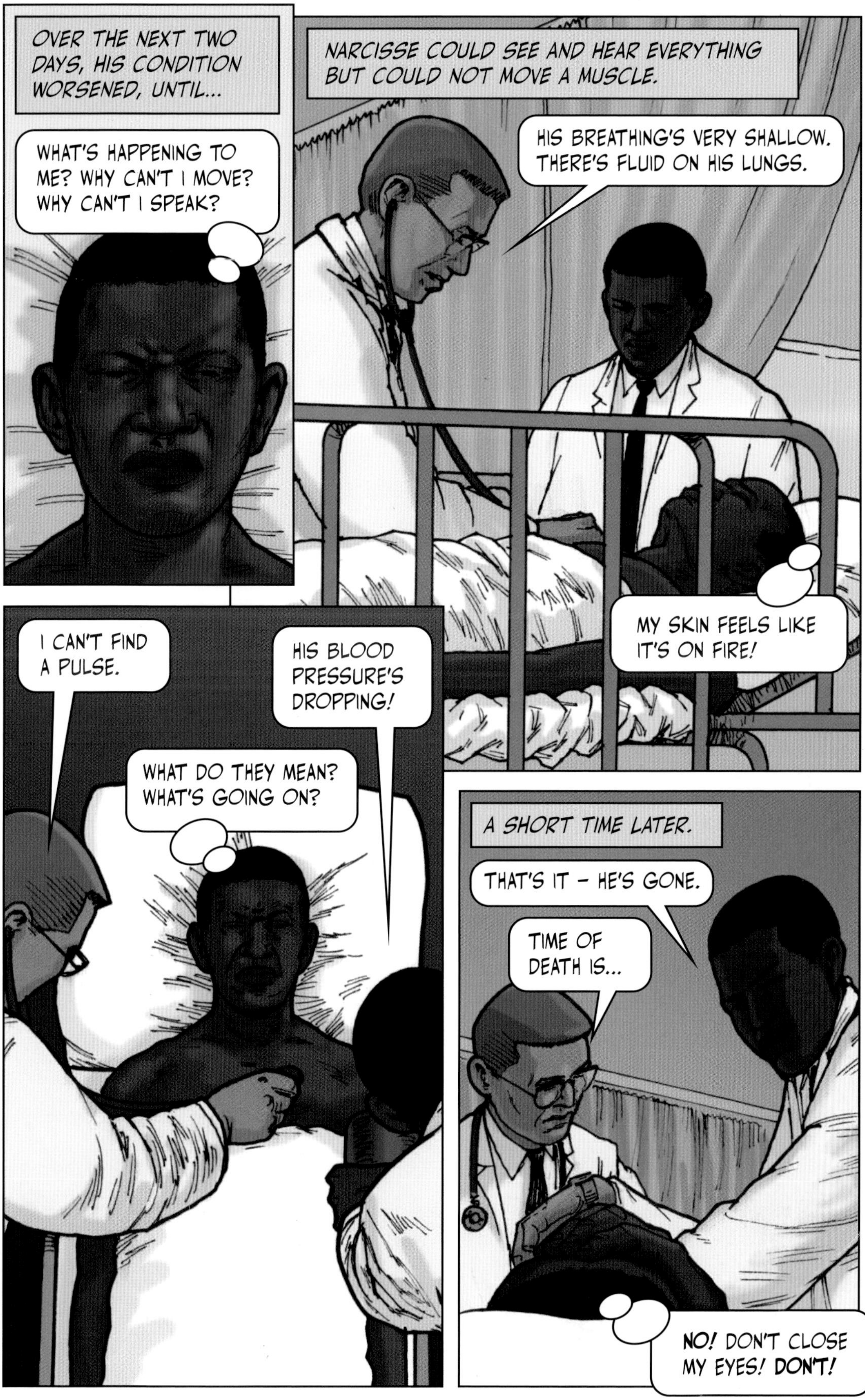
OVER THE NEXT TWO DAYS, HIS CONDITION WORSENED, UNTIL...
WHAT'S HAPPENING TO ME? WHY CAN'T I MOVE? WHY CAN'T I SPEAK?
NARCISSE COULD SEE AND HEAR EVERYTHING BUT COULD NOT MOVE A MUSCLE.
HIS BREATHING'S VERY SHALLOW. THERE'S FLUID ON HIS LUNGS.
MY SKIN FEELS LIKE IT'S ON FIRE!
I CAN'T FIND A PULSE.
HIS BLOOD PRESSURE'S DROPPING!
WHAT DO THEY MEAN? WHAT'S GOING ON?
A SHORT TIME LATER.
THAT'S IT – HE'S GONE.
TIME OF DEATH IS...
NO! DON'T CLOSE MY EYES! DON'T!

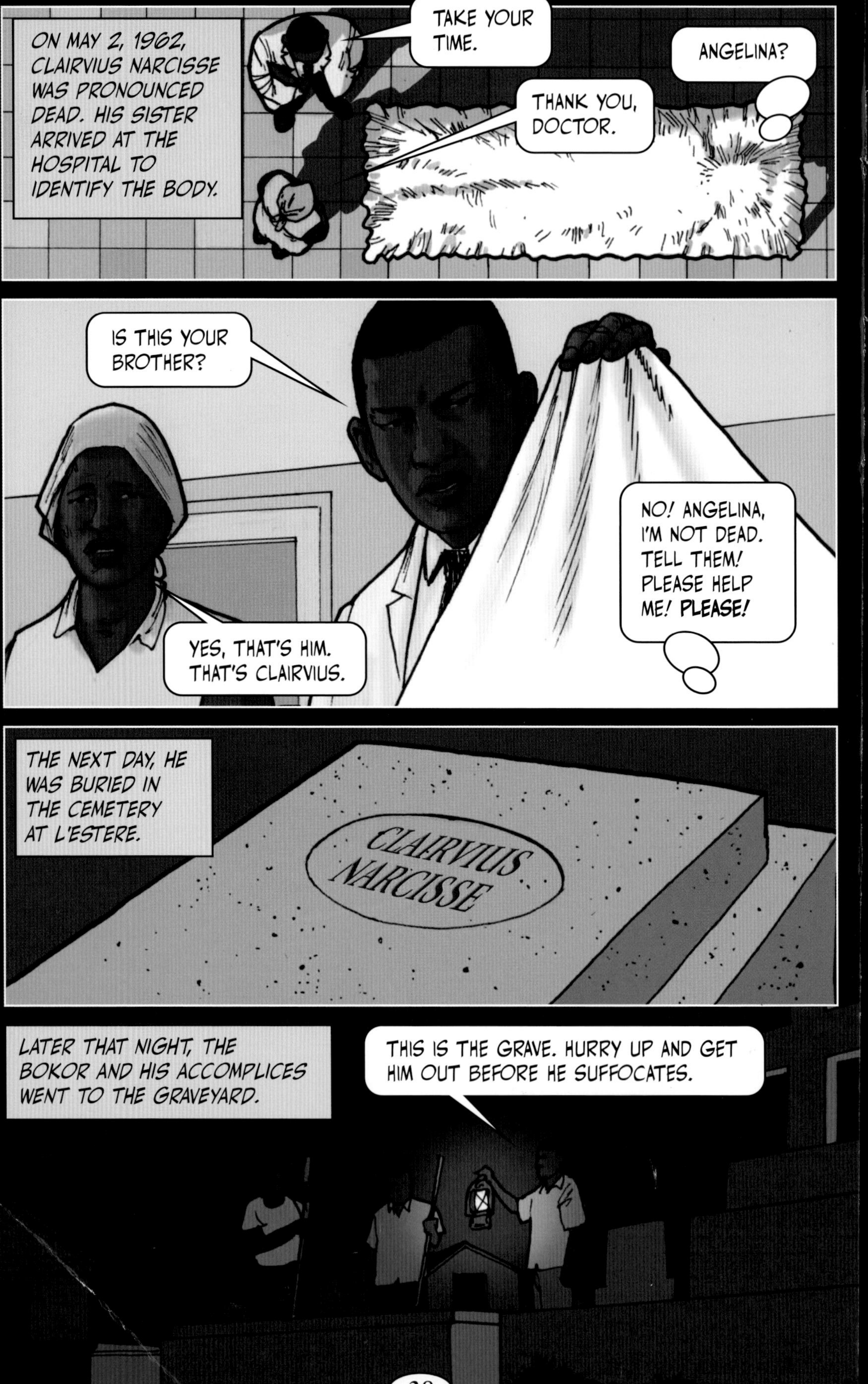
ON MAY 2, 1962, CLAIRVIUS NARCISSE WAS PRONOUNCED DEAD. HIS SISTER ARRIVED AT THE HOSPITAL TO IDENTIFY THE BODY.
TAKE YOUR TIME.
THANK YOU, DOCTOR.
ANGELINA?
IS THIS YOUR BROTHER?
YES, THAT'S HIM. THAT'S CLAIRVIUS.
NO! ANGELINA, I'M NOT DEAD. TELL THEM! PLEASE HELP ME! PLEASE!
THE NEXT DAY, HE WAS BURIED IN THE CEMETERY AT L'ESTERE.
CLAIRVIUS NARCISSE
LATER THAT NIGHT, THE BOKOR AND HIS ACCOMPLICES WENT TO THE GRAVEYARD.
THIS IS THE GRAVE. HURRY UP AND GET HIM OUT BEFORE HE SUFFOCATES.

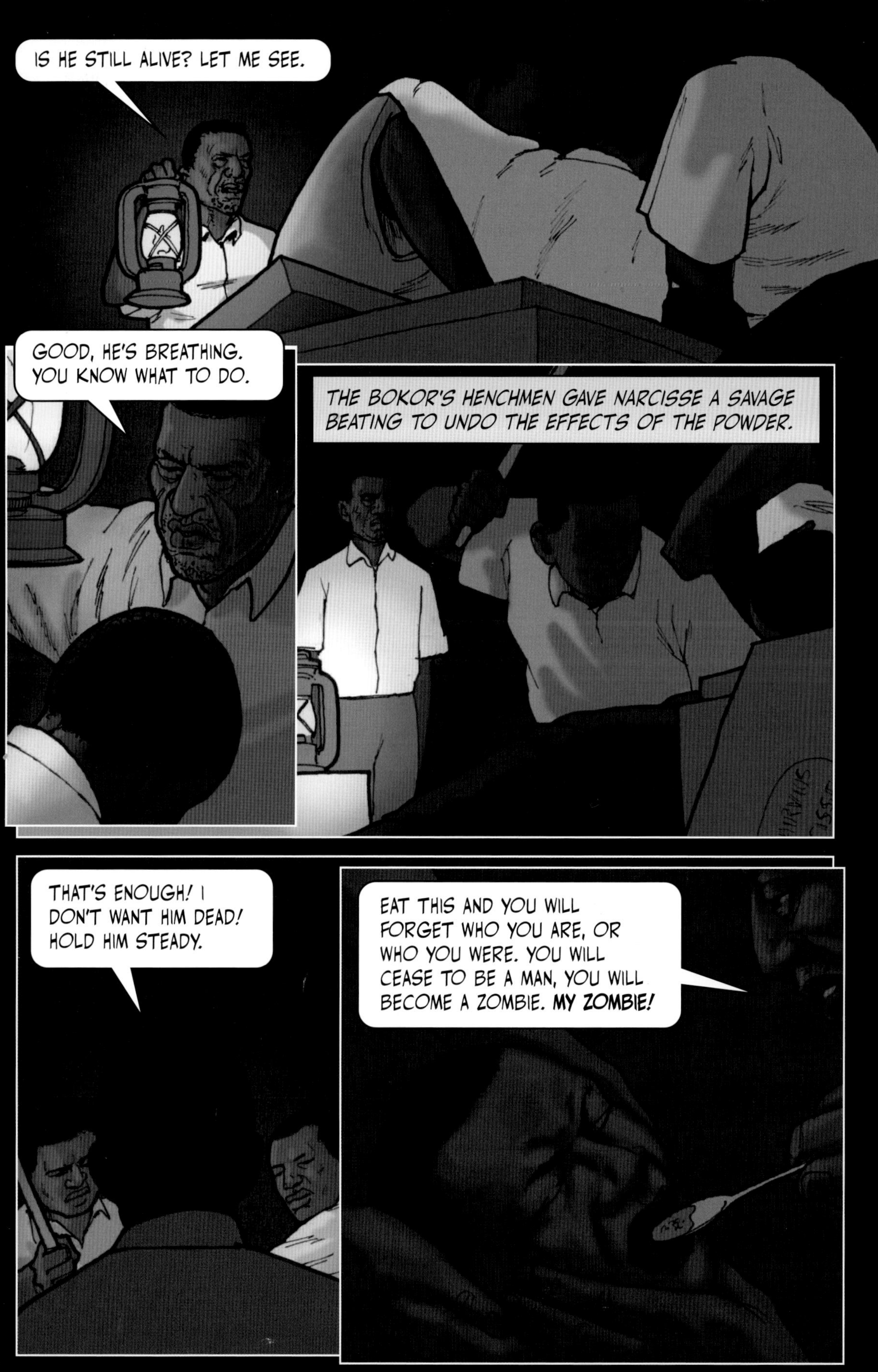
IS HE STILL ALIVE? LET ME SEE.
GOOD, HE'S BREATHING. YOU KNOW WHAT TO DO.
THE BOKOR'S HENCHMEN GAVE NARCISSE A SAVAGE BEATING TO UNDO THE EFFECTS OF THE POWDER.
THAT'S ENOUGH! I DON'T WANT HIM DEAD! HOLD HIM STEADY.
EAT THIS AND YOU WILL FORGET WHO YOU ARE, OR WHO YOU WERE. YOU WILL CEASE TO BE A MAN, YOU WILL BECOME A ZOMBIE. **MY ZOMBIE!**

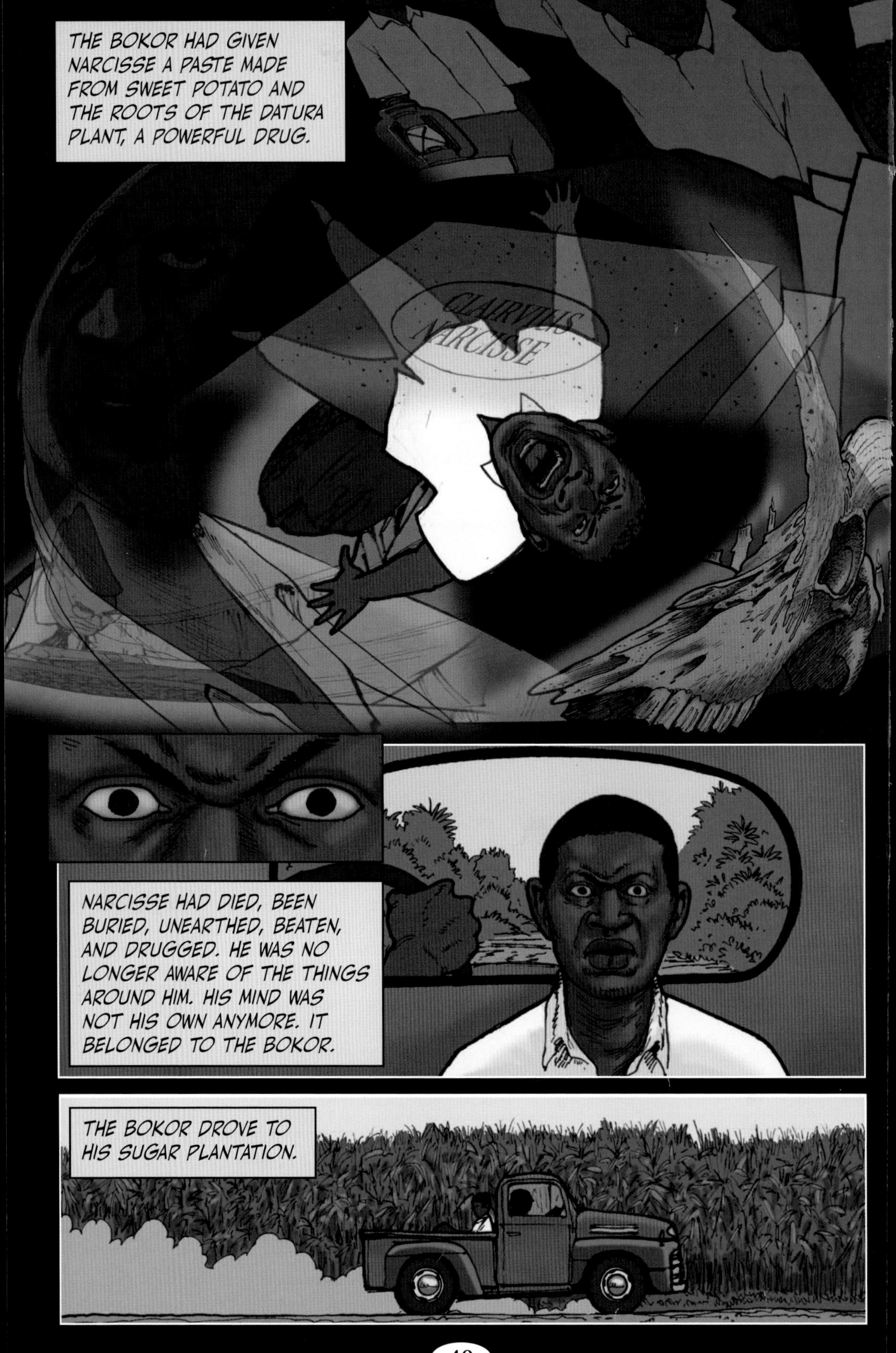
THE BOKOR HAD GIVEN NARCISSE A PASTE MADE FROM SWEET POTATO AND THE ROOTS OF THE DATURA PLANT, A POWERFUL DRUG.
CLAIRVIUS NARCISSE
NARCISSE HAD DIED, BEEN BURIED, UNEARTHED, BEATEN, AND DRUGGED. HE WAS NO LONGER AWARE OF THE THINGS AROUND HIM. HIS MIND WAS NOT HIS OWN ANYMORE. IT BELONGED TO THE BOKOR.
THE BOKOR DROVE TO HIS SUGAR PLANTATION.

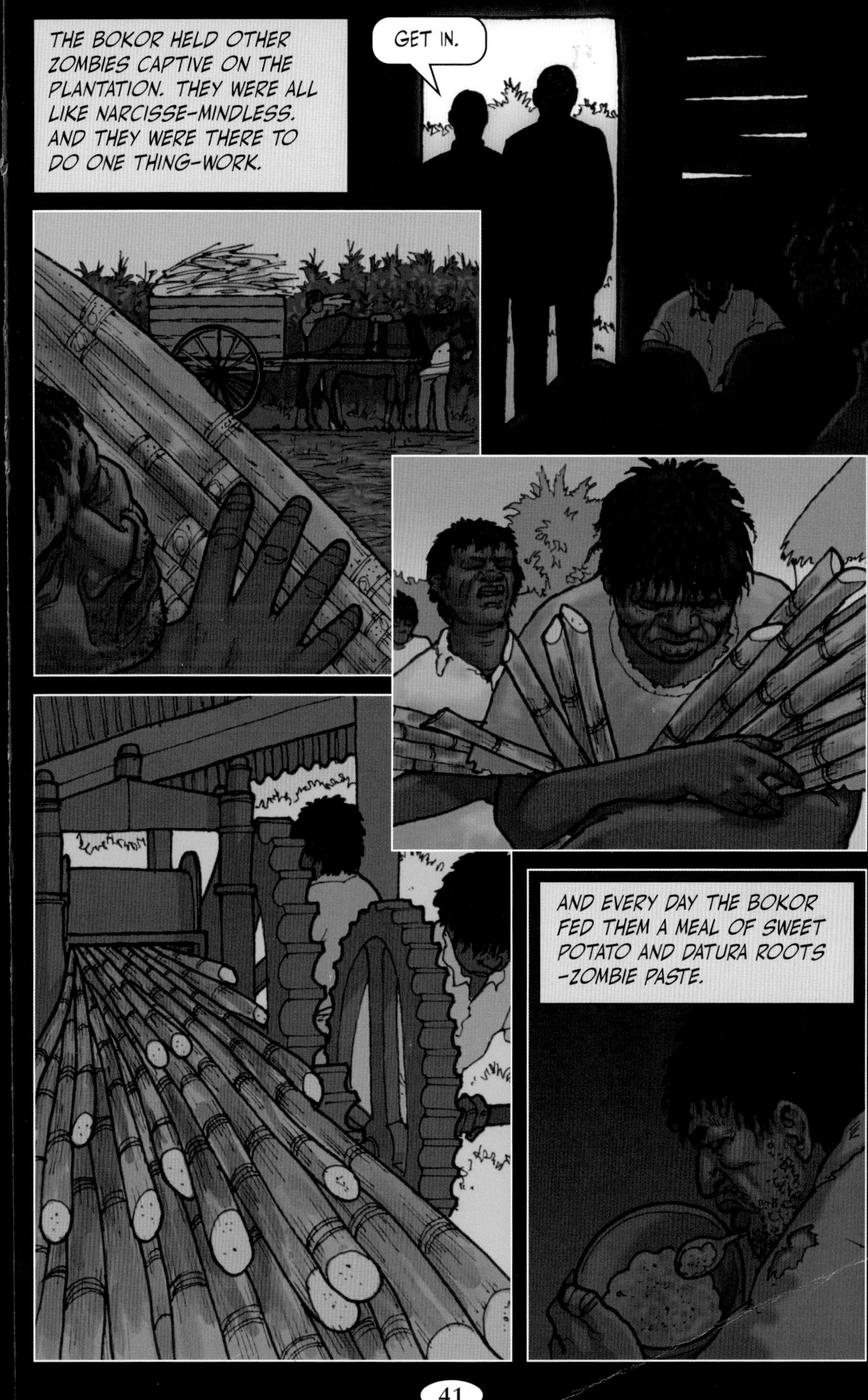
THE BOKOR HELD OTHER ZOMBIES CAPTIVE ON THE PLANTATION. THEY WERE ALL LIKE NARCISSE-MINDLESS. AND THEY WERE THERE TO DO ONE THING-WORK.
GET IN.
AND EVERY DAY THE BOKOR FED THEM A MEAL OF SWEET POTATO AND DATURA ROOTS -ZOMBIE PASTE.

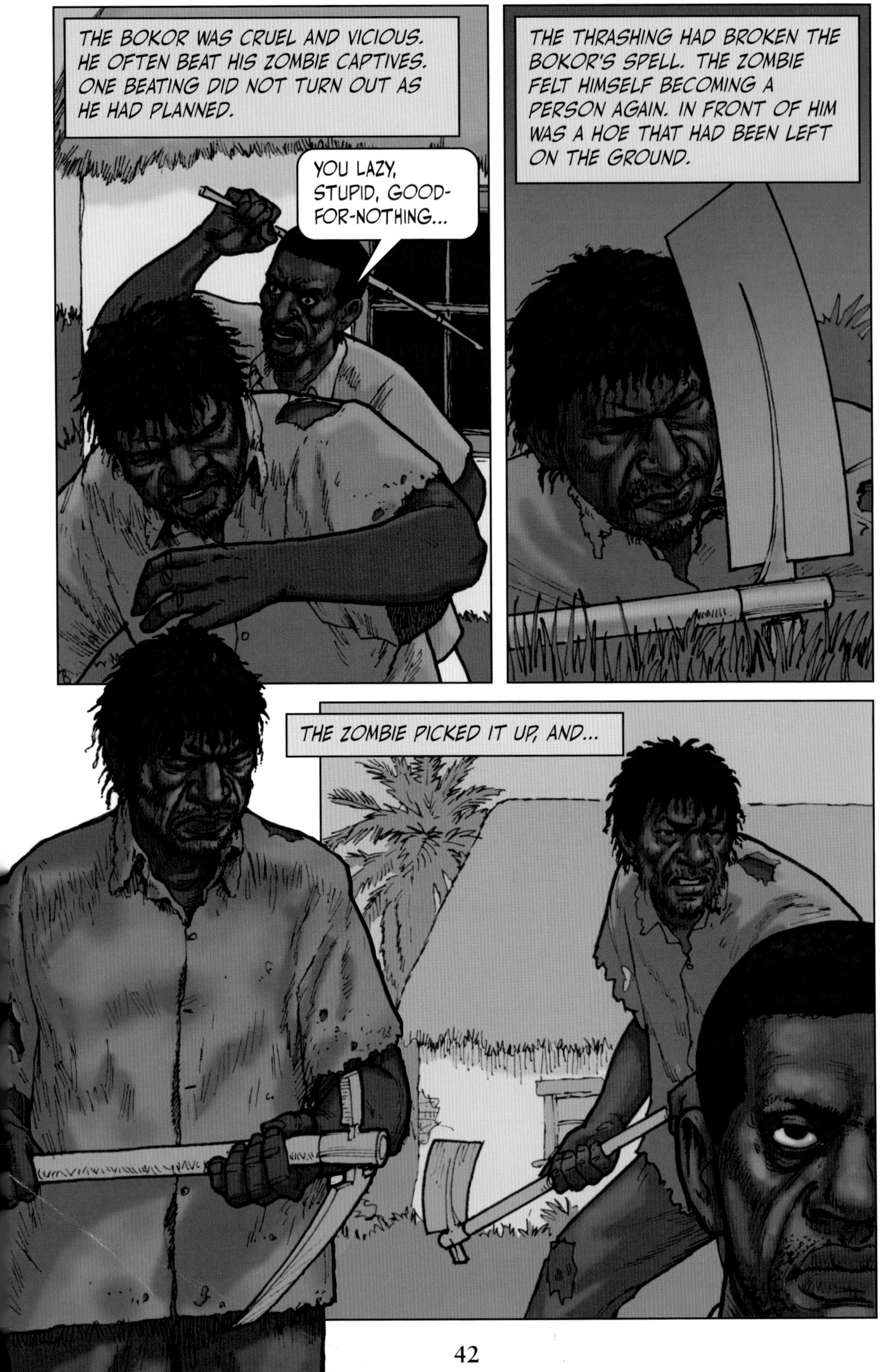
THE BOKOR WAS CRUEL AND VICIOUS. HE OFTEN BEAT HIS ZOMBIE CAPTIVES. ONE BEATING DID NOT TURN OUT AS HE HAD PLANNED.
YOU LAZY, STUPID, GOOD-FOR-NOTHING...
THE THRASHING HAD BROKEN THE BOKOR'S SPELL. THE ZOMBIE FELT HIMSELF BECOMING A PERSON AGAIN. IN FRONT OF HIM WAS A HOE THAT HAD BEEN LEFT ON THE GROUND.
THE ZOMBIE PICKED IT UP, AND...

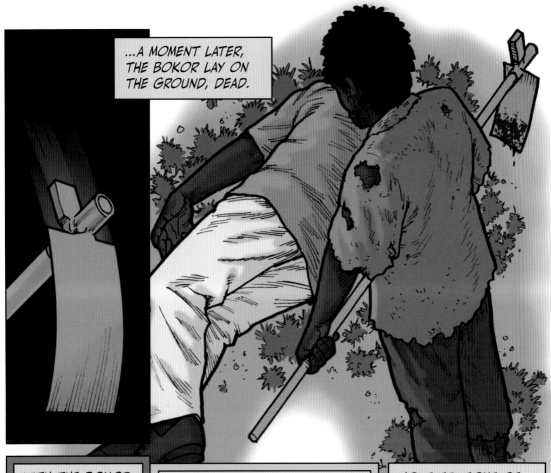

...A MOMENT LATER, THE BOKOR LAY ON THE GROUND, DEAD.

WITH THE BOKOR GONE, THERE WAS NO ONE TO GIVE THE ZOMBIES THE DATURA PASTE. THEY GRADUALLY RECOVERED FROM THEIR TRANCE-LIKE STATE.

CLAIRVIUS NARCISSE ESCAPED FROM THE PLANTATION. HE HAD BEEN UNDER THE BOKOR'S CONTROL FOR TWO YEARS. IT WOULD BE ANOTHER SIXTEEN BEFORE HE FOUND HIS WAY BACK HOME TO L'ESTERE MARKET AND HIS SISTER ANGELINA.

HOWEVER, SOME OF THE CAPTIVES HAD BEEN FED THE PASTE FOR TOO LONG AND THEIR MINDS HAD BEEN DESTROYED. THEY WERE DOOMED TO SPEND THE REST OF THEIR LIVES AS ZOMBIES.

THE END

MORE STORIES OF THE UNDEAD

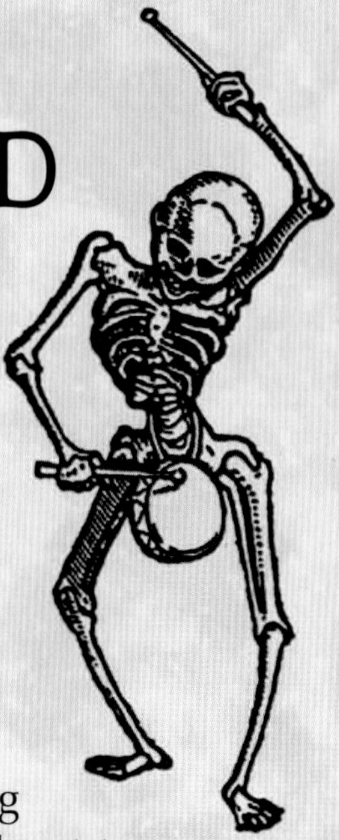

Here are three more terrifying tales of the undead to fill the heart with dread and the veins with ice.

Ola and the Draugr

Ola looked up and froze. He had gone into his boathouse to get a keg of ale. There, sitting on the barrel of beer, was a draugr–an undead monster in human form but with a head of seaweed. Luckily for Ola the draugr was gazing out to sea and had not noticed him. Ola was about to tiptoe away when he suddenly had a playful urge. He crept up behind the draugr and with a sharp shove pushed the creature through the boathouse window and into the sea. The sea boiled and hissed as the draugr hit the water. Ola did not look to admire his handiwork, but turned and fled from the building instead.

The draugr, white hot with rage, flew from the water in pursuit. Ola raced through the village and into the churchyard just out of reach of the draugr's grasping claws. "Rise up all you dead souls and help me!" Ola cried. The ground around him started to tremble, and from the tombs and graves emerged the ghosts of long dead sailors, each one gripping a coffin lid. Ola kept on running and did not see what happened next, but from behind him came the sounds of fighting.

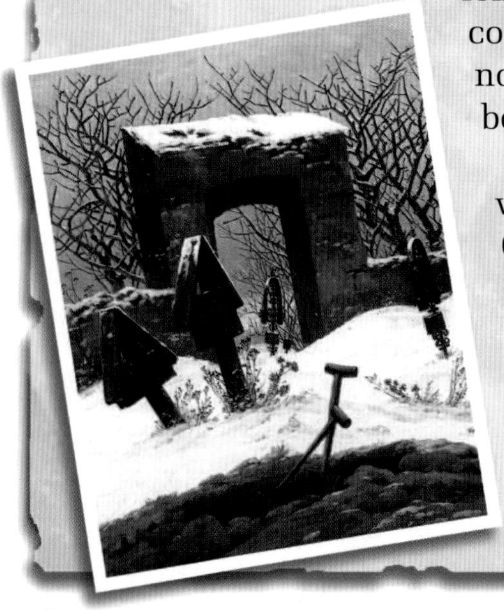

The next morning Ola and the villagers went to church to celebrate Christmas Day. They saw that all the gravestones in the churchyard were draped with rotting seaweed, and shattered coffin lids littered the ground. The sailor ghosts must have won the battle, because the draugr was never seen again.

The Vrykolaka of Santorini

Before he died, Ianettis begged his wife
to pay off his debts. He was a merchant
on the Greek island of Santorini, and
had been trying to settle all his bills.

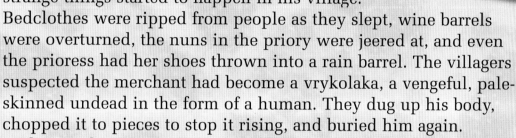

Not long after the merchant's death,
strange things started to happen in his village.
Bedclothes were ripped from people as they slept, wine barrels
were overturned, the nuns in the priory were jeered at, and even
the prioress had her shoes thrown into a rain barrel. The villagers
suspected the merchant had become a vrykolaka, a vengeful, pale-
skinned undead in the form of a human. They dug up his body,
chopped it to pieces to stop it rising, and buried him again.

The attacks continued, though. No one knew why until the wife
came forward. She admitted that she had not carried out her
husband's last wishes and that he had become a vrykolaka. As
soon as all the debts had been paid, the village was left in peace.

The Bokor's Wife

The bokor was sure he had done the right thing. The trip away
could not be avoided, and he had left his farm in the hands of his
young wife. "She has a good head on her shoulders," he thought.
"She won't do anything stupid."

The bokor's wife looked around the farm. It was large and
successful; her husband had many zombies working for him.
She was about to give them their daily meal. "What did my
husband tell me?" she thought, "What must I never feed them?"

She felt sorry for the zombies as they shuffled slowly towards
her. "They deserve a treat." She went into the farmhouse and
came out with a jar of sweet pimento peppers. "These will
cheer them up!" she said to herself. The zombies each pulled a
pepper from the jar and popped them into their mouths.
As they chewed the red fruit, the expressions in their eyes
changed. Suddenly they could remember what had happened to
them. Just as suddenly, they all fell to the ground, dead.
"Salt!" cried the bokor's wife. "That's what they shouldn't eat!"
The pimentos had been soaked in salt water, which had broken
the bokor's spell. The zombies were all human again—and had
died for a second time.

GLOSSARY

bokor Voodoo priest.

cell A small room.

corpse The body of a dead person.

crevice A crack forming an opening.

crypt A room beneath a church used as a chapel or burial place.

desperate Having an urgent need or desire.

distrust To regard with doubt, to have no trust in.

grove A small forested area.

Haiti West Indies country on the western half of the island Hispaniola.

haul Something that is obtained.

Hessians Mercenaries from the region of Hesse in Germany.

highwayman Someone, especially someone on horseback, who robbed travelers on public roads.

hogwash Meaningless talk, nonsense.

hurtle To move with great speed.

mummy A dead body preserved by specific chemical treatments.

prioress A nun in charge of a priory.

priory A monastery or convent headed by a prior or prioress.

root out To remove completely.

scopolamine A drug produced by certain plants, including Datura, used to treat motion sickness, can cause confusion and hallucinations.

shroud A sheet of cloth used to wrap up a dead body.

spurs Devices attached to a rider's shoes, used to urge a horse forward.

suffocate To kill by preventing breathing.

tavern A place where alcohol is sold and drunk.

terrorize To produce widespread fear by acts of violence.

tetrodotoxin A poison produced by some puffer fish, can cause heart failure and affect breathing.

trudge To walk tiredly.

victim A person who suffers from violence.

Voodoo A religion derived from Catholicism and African spiritualism.

wicked Evil or sinful.

FOR MORE INFORMATION

ORGANIZATIONS

How Stuff Works: Zombies
http://science.howstuffworks.com/science-vs-myth/strange-creatures/zombie.htm

FOR FURTHER READING

Barnhill, Kelly Regan. *Blood-Sucking, Man-Eating Monsters.* Mankato, MN: Capstone Publishing, 2009.

Ganeri, Anita. *An Illustrated Guide to Mythical Creatures.* New York, NY: Hammond, 2009.

Ganeri, Anita. *Vampires and the Undead* (The Dark Side). New York, NY: PowerKids Press, 2011.

Kresnsky, Stephen. *Zombies.* Minneapolis, MN: Lerner Publishing Group, 2008.

Rooney, Anne. *Zombies on the Loose.* New York, NY: Crabtree Publishing Company, 2008.

Schuh, Mari C. *Zombies.* Mankato, MN: Capstone Publishers, 2007.

Whiting, Jim. *Scary Monsters.* Mankato, MN: Capstone Publishing, 2010.

INDEX

Web Sites

Due to the changing nature of Internet links, Rosen Publishing has developed an online list of Web sites related to the subject of this book. This site is updated regularly. Please use this link to access the list:

http://www.rosenlinks.com/gts/zomb